WOLFKILLER

AS RECORDED BY
LOUISA WADE WETHERILL

COMPILED BY
HARVEY LEAKE

WOLFKILLER

WISDOM FROM A NINETEENTH-CENTURY NAVAJO SHEPHERD

Gibbs Smith, Publisher
TO ENRICH AND INSPIRE HUMANKIND
Salt Lake City | Charleston | Santa Fe | Santa Barbara

First Edition
16 15 14 13 12 5 4 3 2

Published by
Gibbs Smith, Publisher
PO Box 667
Layton, Utah 84041

Orders: 1.800.835.4993
www.gibbs-smith.com

Designed by Jody Billert
Printed and bound in Canada

Library of Congress Cataloging-in-Publication Data

Wolfkiller.
Wolfkiller : wisdom from a nineteenth-century Navajo Shepherd / recorded by Louisa Wade Wetherill ; compiled by Harvey Leake. — 1st ed.
p. cm.
ISBN-13: 978-1-4236-0030-5
ISBN-10: 1-4236-0030-4
1. Wolfkiller. 2. Navajo Indians—Monument Valley (Ariz. and Utah)—Biography. 3. Shepherds—Monument Valley (Ariz. and Utah)—Biography. 4. Navajo Indians—Monument Valley (Ariz. and Utah)—Social life and customs. 5. Monument Valley (Ariz. and Utah)—History. I. Wetherill, Louisa Wade. II. Leake, Harvey. III. Title.

E99.N3W735 2007
979.2'59—dc22
[B]

2006027358

CONTENTS

PREFACE

By Harvey Leake

Found among the papers of my great-grandmother, Louisa Wade Wetherill, was this remarkable story of early Navajo life told to her by her elderly friend, Wolfkiller.

Louisa and her husband, John, lived among the Navajos for more than forty years, beginning in New Mexico in 1900. In 1906, when they announced their plans to move to the Monument Valley region of southern Utah to operate a trading post, their friends and relatives warned them against it. The inhabitants of that region were dangerous, uncivilized renegades, they were told. To the contrary, the Wetherills found their new neighbors to be hospitable, generous, and sometimes wise to a degree rarely found among "civilized" folks.

One of the wisest was the kindly Wolfkiller. He tells the story of his upbringing in this book. He describes the sage advice of his grandfather and mother that led him through hard times with grace, wit, and honor. They taught him to look to his natural surroundings for the most important lessons and helped him to appreciate even the wind, storm, and cold. These insights enabled him to face life, as well as death, with optimism and courage.

Wolfkiller and Louisa Wade Wetherill collaborated on the writing of *Wolfkiller* over a period of several years. Wolfkiller told his story in Navajo, and Louisa, who had an exceptional command of the Navajo language, translated it into English using "the simple language in which he related the many incidents and stories to me." My great-grandmother stated that she did not have the benefit of a stenographer, and I have found no evidence that anyone else was involved in the preparation of the manuscript. Considering that neither my great-grandmother nor Wolfkiller was an experienced writer, the continuity of the text and its

Wolfkiller, ca 1855–1926.

depth of meaning attest to Wolfkiller's abilities as a master storyteller and philosopher.

Only minor changes were needed to improve the flow of the present work. There were some grammatical and punctuation corrections, and chapter breaks and titles were added. Navajo words were updated to their modern spellings and their translations were clarified based on invaluable input from Dr. Robert W. Young of the University of New Mexico (if there are any errors, however, they are my own).

Louisa's introduction, portions of which follow this preface, was the result of a request made by a prospective publisher prior to his rejection of the book. He asked her to tell about her own background among the Navajos. "I had hoped to have kept this from being any part of myself," she protested. To honor her original intention, I have retained only the parts of the introduction needed to set the stage for Wolfkiller's story. Most of the omitted information is available in a different format in *Traders to the Navajos,* by Frances Gillmor and Louisa Wade Wetherill, which is a book about my great-grandmother's own experiences.

Traders to the Navajos also includes Wolfkiller's account of his sister's coming-of-age ceremony. Since this account has already been published and does not seem to relate to the central theme of Wolfkiller's story, I omitted it from the present work.

When Louisa completed the manuscript in 1932, civilized society was not ready for it. A prospective publisher found portions of the story difficult to believe. "You say that Wolfkiller discussed the injustice of life with his brother," he wrote. "I doubt very much whether a child of six would talk or know of such problems. It would be better to make the boy about twelve or fourteen."

For many decades the manuscript remained hidden in the family archives until it was recently rediscovered and recognized as offering a unique and profound alternative to modern culture's compulsive attempt to escape from nature. Although Wolfkiller and Mrs. Wetherill are long gone, here, finally, is their story.

Louisa Wade Wetherill, 1877–1945.

Louisa Wade Wetherill and Wolfkiller in about 1924 when they were nearing completion of the book.

INTRODUCTION

By Louisa Wade Wetherill

I first met Wolfkiller in 1906 at Oljato (Moonlight Water), in southeastern Utah. Oljato, at that time, was one of the most remote places in the country. The nearest town was seventy miles away, access to the area was difficult, and few outsiders ventured that way. The Navajos and Piutes who lived there still kept to their old customs, little affected by white society. None of them spoke English.

The residents of the Oljato region lived in hogans, which are conical-shaped houses made of poles covered with bark and mud. The doorways face the sunrise, and a blanket is used as a door to keep out the blowing sand and cold. The only other opening is a smoke hole at the apex of the roof. Around the hearth, the packed-dirt floor is carpeted with sheepskins and robes, making for a pleasant and cozy place to gather on cold evenings.

A old-style hogan. Forked logs are interlocked at the apex to form a cone shape, and then smaller logs and sticks are added and covered with mud. The only openings are the door, which always faces east, and the smoke hole in the roof.

The Navajos who lived there still dressed in the old style. The men wore pants made of bed ticking or unbleached white muslin, and the women skirts of calico—usually two or three layers thick. Their shirts and blouses were made of velveteen, leggings and moccasins of buckskin, and jewelry of silver, coral, white shell, and turquoise. Colorful robes of handwoven wool or Pendleton blankets completed the outfit.

Five years earlier, my husband, two children, and I had moved to the badlands of northwestern New Mexico to run the Ojo Alamo trading post. It was there that I began to learn about Navajo language and customs.

At first I found it disconcerting to live in surroundings that were so different from the verdant Mancos Valley of southwestern Colorado where I grew up. New Mexico looked barren and forbidding, and our new neighbors were hard to understand.

My perspective changed suddenly one day when a man invited me to see a sandpainting. I did not expect to see very much, but when I stepped inside his hogan, I got the surprise of my life. There, on the floor, was a painting made just of sand. It was beautiful! In it were mountains, birds, antelope, corn, beans, pumpkins, and a plant the Navajos call "mountain tobacco," made of red, blue, black, yellow, and white sands. To look at the surrounding country, you would not think they could find so many different vivid colors, but they are there.

I decided then that I must learn as much as possible about the Navajos. After I gained their confidence, they helped me as much as they could. I asked them many questions. The old people explained their ceremonies and chants, which were quite incomprehensible to me at first. After much hard study, I eventually came to understand that they all have a logical purpose.

After my five-year initiation among the Navajos of New Mexico, I wanted to go where the Indians still lived in their old ways. That is why, in 1906, we decided to move to Oljato, Utah, where the Navajos and Piutes reigned supreme. We heard a good many warnings about their misdeeds, but those stories did not daunt us. We were not afraid of the Navajos, and we did not think we would have any trouble with the Piutes.

We left New Mexico in a little caravan loaded with all our earthly possessions, as well as goods to trade with the Indians. My husband, John, drove a wagon; I drove a buggy; and our two children, Ben (age nine) and Georgia Ida (age seven), who we called Sister, rode horseback.

Preparation for a sandpainting ceremony. The medicine man and his assistants are applying colored sands to the smoothed hogan floor to make intricate pictures. Sunlight through the smoke hole provides natural light.

The journey was a long and difficult one. We struggled through mud, sand, and roadless stretches for much of the way.

On the nineteenth day, our progress was halted by a deep arroyo, with steep cutbanks. After surveying the situation, we estimated that it would take us two days of hard work to build a route across it. Suddenly, while we were still contemplating our predicament, we saw Navajo men, women, and children walking toward us from all directions. They were not the least bit hostile, but were all very friendly. After we ate lunch together, the men helped us build the road. In just half a day it was passable, and we were so grateful to be able to camp on the other side that night. We knew then that we were going to like our new friends.

The next day we reached Oljato. We chose a flat spot on a sandy rise above the water hole where we set up tents and a temporary trading post, which was just a board across two coffee boxes. We then started building a permanent house and trading post. Several Navajo men cut timbers for us and helped with the construction.

Among the workers was one man we particularly noticed. He was very quiet and always smiled. He never participated in the arguments that sometimes came up among the other workers, but just went about his own business, paying no attention to what might irritate the others. With his earnings, he bought clothing and food for his family, while some of the other men gambled most of their money away. They called him Wolfkiller.

Sister Wetherill, daughter of Louisa, with a Navajo friend at Oljato. The Wetherills and their Indian helpers had to improvise when they built the house and trading post. Wood from Arbuckles coffee crates was used to construct the gate.

Mrs. Wetherill's Navajo friends called her "Slim Woman." The two wooden structures are guards to protect saplings, which the Wetherills had planted, from hungry livestock.

After watching him for a while, I began to ask Wolfkiller questions. He told me who the other people were and where they lived, but what he said about them was always good. He never had anything bad to say about anyone.

One day a medicine man came in and asked him to gather some plants for a medicine ceremony. We asked some of the other Navajos why he was chosen for this job, and they explained that he was a medicine-gatherer and knew more about plants than anyone else did. This interested me very much, and I determined to learn more about the subject.

We lived at Oljato for nearly five years. Then, in 1910, we moved thirty miles south to Kayenta, Arizona, where most of the Navajos who traded with us lived. Wolfkiller worked for us there, and we talked to each other almost every day. He told me these stories of his upbringing and how the lessons of his grandfather and mother had helped him throughout his life.

One day he explained why they called him Wolfkiller. "I was camping alone one night near the brink of a canyon that runs into the San Juan River when a wolf came near my camp and howled. You know we are afraid of wolves. I did not want to let my fears get the better of me, so I made myself think of pleasant things. I built a big fire and tried to stay awake, but when I would doze off, he would howl again. I knew we were not supposed to shoot a wolf, but when it was almost morning, I decided to kill him because he had annoyed me all night. I shot him, and he fell down into the canyon. I sat by the fire until it was light enough for me to see, and then climbed down to take a look. Soon I found him, but I discovered that he was not a wolf—he was a man dressed in the skin of a wolf. I went home and told my people what I had done. They said they knew who the man was and that he had been frightening them for some time. They thought he was insane and were glad I had killed him, as now they would not be worried about what he would do to them."

I asked Wolfkiller how a person such as the wolf imposter could harm another person without touching him. "It is the fear that is put into the mind of one of us by the evil thought of another," he answered.

"But how can just a thought do any harm?" I asked. He seemed surprised that I did not realize that a thought could have much power, even though it was unexpressed. "A thought, whether spoken or not, is a real thing," he explained. "Don't you know that if someone is very ill and the medicine man is trying to cure him, there must not be anyone around whose thoughts are working against the medicine man? No one must say or think anything but good. No one must think that the patient will not recover. If someone among us does not have faith, the work is all lost. We must all believe that our prayers will be answered and that all will be peace. I would never have thought anything about the sorrows an evil thought can cause if my grandfather had not taught me as he did."

I discussed this concept with some of the other old men, and they all said the same thing. They were concerned that some of the younger people were beginning to express doubt in this faith, and that, if they did not change soon, the people would soon be lost. "As long as we old people live, we will try to keep our children following the path of light as we see it," said one of the elders.

To help the younger people along their way, Wolfkiller agreed that I should record his story. Through many winter evenings he narrated it to me, and I translated and transcribed it.

PART I—EDUCATION

The Path of Light

When I was a young boy, about six years old, my grandfather and mother started me on the path of light.

One morning, early in the spring, my mother asked my brother and me to take the sheep out to feed. The wind was blowing hard, and we were angry that we had to leave the hogan fire and go out into the cold.

We herded the sheep over to the nearest place we could find greasewood for them to eat—a big, flat area where some brush was growing along the banks of a deep wash. To get out of the wind, we climbed down into the wash, leaving our sheep and burro with the big blue dog to guard them.

We sat there and talked about the injustice of life—how we had to leave the nice warm hogan to herd the sheep while other children could stay at home and have a good time. Our mother and sister got to stay inside where it was warm, with nothing to do but cook and weave blankets.

"I wish the Spaniards and white men had never come to our land," I complained. "They have brought us nothing but trouble. They brought these nasty, woolly beasts for us to herd, so we have to go out in the wind, snow, rain, and hot sun to herd them. They must always be followed every place, no matter what happens. We would be so much happier if these people had never come among us. Think how nice it would be if we could just sit around the hogan fire, listening to stories the men tell of their deer hunts and fights with the Utes and Apaches. In the old days, the little boys had nothing to do but wait until they grew up so they could go out and hunt and steal wives from the Pueblos."

Just then, we heard our grandfather on the bank above. We sat very still, hoping he would not know where we were, but very soon we heard him climbing down the bank toward us. We were quite afraid that he would punish us in some way, but when we saw his face, we knew he was not angry.

He came and sat down by us and spoke very quietly.

I was riding across the flat over there, hunting my horses, when I saw the sheep feeding, and the burro standing with his head down and his tail to the wind. I looked for you boys, but could see nothing of you. I thought you would be watching the sheep, but I saw no one with them except the big blue dog. He is a very faithful dog and seems to be contented. I guess you did not hear me ride up. I decided you were down here out of the wind, letting someone else do your work.

I wondered what you would be doing, so I slipped up and lay down on the bank to listen to you. I heard you say that you wished the white people had never come to our land and had never brought these nasty, woolly sheep. You wished you could lie around the hogan fire until you were grown up. You were saying how much nicer it was when our people had nothing to do but hunt, fight the Utes and Apaches, and steal women from the Pueblos.

You have heard only one side of the story. You have not heard of the times when the hunters went out, but found few deer and had to come home nearly empty-handed. You have not heard of the times when we had to dig roots and gather a few berries to keep life in our bodies through the long winter months. We had to camp under any kind of a shelter that could be built, with few robes to keep us warm. You have not heard of the times when we went out to gather the yucca fruit and dry it for our winter's food, and how we had to guard our camps day and night for fear that the Utes would come to steal all our women and children to sell or keep as slaves for themselves. You have not heard how mothers with young babies died because they could not feed two people on what would have been too little for one, and, when the mother died, how the old women kept the tiny babies alive on the broth from dried meat and the juice from the inner bark of the cedar. You have not heard of the time when our people went out to gather pinyon nuts, and at night had to build their camps on poles in a tree to keep the wolves from getting them. These are only a few of the hardships our people have gone through.

There have been times in our past when the people have suffered more than I can tell you—times when we had more enemies than we could count. All the tribes seemed to be against us. Our people were in hiding for moons and moons. We could not camp anywhere near water, as that is where the trails lead. Our hogans, as you know, are built to look just like another mound of earth, but we could not have fire enough to keep warm or cook our food in them, for fear that a traveling party would smell the smoke and find us.

We did not have these nasty, woolly beasts you hate so much to furnish us with meat or their wool to make clothes of. Often in those times, we had nothing for clothing but cedar bark and sticky mud to keep our bodies from freezing. Sometimes, when we could get out into the open for long enough, we gathered yucca to strip down and pound into fiber to weave into clothing.

Then, when the tribes were all against us, and the earth was nothing but evil thoughts of war and greed, the years came when the rain did not fall. The sun was very hot and the wind blew day after day, year after year, for seven years. The corn dried up and the grass did not come, the deer and antelope scattered, and many of them died of thirst and starvation. Although the people were full of evil thoughts, we had no war for the time, as everyone was busy trying to find food enough to keep life in their skeletons, which was about all that was left of them.

The old men talked among themselves and decided to have some ceremonies to get the people's minds working in the right direction. They called the people together and told them of their decision. 'We have been having nothing but trouble for many long years, and now we are being punished for our sins,' the old men said. 'It has been always so. When we are not satisfied with what comes to us, when we are well and strong and have food, we think things will come to us without any effort on our part. But nothing comes to anyone that is not paid for. If we want the good things of life, we must work for them. The anger and evil thoughts in our hearts are what have caused us all of our trouble. We know that anger is the worst sin, as it leads to all kinds of evil thought, and we know that evil thought is just a black path that leads us nowhere but into the dark. The path of light is always running beside us on either side, but we cannot see it for the darkness in our hearts. Now we have decided to have some ceremonies and pray for our minds to turn into the path of light.'

Then the old men began to tell the stories of the early history of the people that had been handed down to them. They told of the time when the people were suffering from hunger, and how they prayed for help, and the next day the ground was covered with white food. For several days, the people were happy again, as the white food gave them strength. But there is always someone who cannot be satisfied. The Coyote Man began to complain about the food and to send out evil thoughts. He said it was too cold. The next day, when the people went out to eat the food, it was just water in their mouths and had no nourishment—it had turned to snow.

For the evil thought of one man, all the people had to suffer. We learned from this that a thought is a thing that can either bring us evil or good. A good thought will bring all of our people good, and an evil thought will bring evil to all.

They told many other stories of sickness, suffering, and death from hunger and war. Then they began their ceremonies. All the people prayed for rain and peace, and they came out of the path of evil thought. Then the rain came, the trees and plants laughed again, and the people had food and clothing.

My brother and I had never heard any of the old people talk like this before. It made us ashamed that we had complained about the wind and the sheep that we had to herd.

Our grandfather then said that he must go and hunt his horse. "I do not expect things to come to me unless I deserve them," he said as he left. "We must give something for everything we receive. I must give up the comfort of the hogan fire and face the wind if I am to find my horse. I have many stories that I think you should hear. Tonight I will come to your hogan and tell you one of them."

We followed him out of the wash and gathered our sheep to herd them to better feed. The wind did not bother us half as much now, although it was blowing even harder. The sheep did not seem so bad to us, either, as the promise of another story gave us something to look forward to. The rest of the day we talked about the things our grandfather had told us.

A shepherd with his flock at the water hole. The Navajos call this small pond *Oljato*, which means "moonlight water." Natural water sources, such as this, are rare in the arid Navajo country.

When evening came, we started the sheep homeward. They traveled slowly, eating as they went, and had to be taken to the water hole on the way home. It took us until sunset to get them back to the stone corral, where we left them to the care of the blue dog for the night. We were glad to finish our chores and to go inside, out of the wind.

Observation

We sat on a sheepskin by the hogan fire while our mother served us our supper of meat, goat's milk, and corn bread. When the dark had come and the fire was burning brightly, our grandfather arrived to tell us the story he had promised us.

"Though the wind is blowing very hard tonight, we are warm and should feel thankful for the blessing of having the sheep you were saying you hated. The sheep are safe in the rocks with the dog to guard them through the night. You boys complain about working through the day, but the dog does not complain although he is always on guard and does not get half the reward you get. You said today that you were doomed to lead a dull life, just going out in the wind, snow, rain, and hot sun to herd sheep. Do you not know that everything about you is interesting if you see things in the right light? Even the burro you were riding today has a story, and I am going to tell it to you."

It was nice and warm in the hogan and all the children and grown people grew silent as Grandfather told us this story.

Creation of the Burro

Many, many years ago, when our people lived in the old houses that are now in ruins, the Creator (*'Atsé Hastiin*) made for them deer, coyotes, antelopes, and many other animals. He made them of pearl, agate, jet, turquoise, and other things. When he finished making them, he had a pile of scraps of medicines, food, jewels, and other things left over. Having no use for these materials, he left them and went to his home.

The chief of the villages had a beautiful little sister who liked to play and make things out of clay. She enjoyed exploring the strange

An elderly Navajo shepherd.

corners of the canyon where she lived. One day, while playing, she found the scraps that the Creator had left after he had finished making the animals. She ran out to hunt her little brother, calling, "Sitsilí, my little brother, my little brother, come and see what I have found! Come and let's play with these beautiful things. Let's see what we can make of them."

She took her brother to the place where the pile of discards was. Picking up a piece of jet, she said, "Let us make some hoofs of this." They cut the jet into four small hoofs. Then they picked up a handful of the small bits of different things and made a nose. Over this, they sprinkled a handful of the ashes of stardust of which the Milky Way was made. That is why your burro has a gray nose now. The children laughed and laughed. "How funny the nose looks, all covered with ashes," they said.

Next, they took a small pile of scraps and molded it into a back, which they sprinkled with ashes and coal. From another pile of scraps they molded a body, and then they made four small legs and attached them all together. To this they added the four small hoofs and some stripes of jet around the legs.

Now they had a very funny looking animal. He had no ears, so they made him some that looked like those of a jackrabbit. From a cattail that was growing nearby, they took some fuzz and pasted it on the body for hair. Then they sprinkled their creation with stardust. He needed a tail, so they made him one out of the material that the Creator had made the little black worms of.

"He has no heart, liver, lungs, or intestines," the little girl said. "We must make him some." So they cut a heart out of a piece of the stone of which red beads are made. They made him a liver of turquoise and lungs of red stones. They made his intestines of white shell and his tongue of all kinds of scraps. He was finished but could not move, so they put a piece of white shell in for a windpipe. Still, he did not move.

"We only made him for a joke anyway," said the little girl. He was a funny looking animal, and they had a lot of fun over him.

Then the wind whispered to them and said, "He is beautiful inside and is made of strong things. I will put breath into him so he will live, as it is not right to waste beautiful things." So the burro stood up and was alive.

Wolfkiller's grandfather told him a story about the children who created the first burro.

The children went out and gathered pollen from all types of plants, and they fed it to the burro. "Now you won't care what you eat," they said. Then the little girl went out and scooped some water into a white shell. She gave it to the burro to drink. He began to bray and made a very funny noise because his tongue was made of many different scraps. The children laughed and laughed and jumped up and down, clapping their hands and saying, "You are truly a joke!"

"You are not very pretty on the outside with your big head, long ears, and funny tail," the little girl said, "but you are beautiful inside, for you are made of beautiful things."

Then the wind whispered to them and said, "You must not say mean things about people if you want them to amount to anything. From now on, you must think and talk about this animal in a kindly way. Think of what he is made of inside and not what he looks like on the outside. You know how it depends on what a person is inside as to whether they are worthwhile or not. From now on, try to find the good in people and do not look for the evil. When one looks for the evil in things, they poison themselves as well as the people around them. If you look for the good, you will help yourselves and the people around you."

The children took the burro out to where all the people of the village were working and called them to come and see what they had made. The people gathered around and made fun of him. They also laughed at the children for making such a funny looking animal. This made the little girl angry.

"If you think he is so ugly, maybe he can run," she said. "Bring on your other animals and let's have a race."

Just to humor the children and have a little fun, the older people smoothed off a racetrack all around the villages. Then they called in all the other animals and told them what was going to happen.

The animals gathered around the little burro and laughed and made all kinds of fun of him, telling him how bad they were going to beat him in the race, for they said that one so ugly as he was—and so small and so slow looking—could not run. The children went over to the burro and told him that he was to run this race, and not to mind what the other animals said, but to do his best. Now this race was to be four times around the villages, and it was a long way from one village to the other.

Finally, everything was ready, so the animals were called to the line, and the race began. The deer, with her long, shapely legs, started away with a bound. Right behind her came the coyote on a long run, and the other animals came rapidly behind them, wanting to get the race over in a hurry so they might laugh more at the funny little burro, who was following along behind at a slow, steady trot.

The first time around the track, the deer, coyote, and other animals were far ahead. When they came around the second time, the little burro was right up with the horses and mules. On the third lap, he passed all the animals except the deer, coyote, and antelope, which he had caught up with. On the final lap, the little burro passed the rest of the animals. They had collapsed alongside the track, tired out. The little burro came in long before the sun went down and did not seem a bit tired. The next day the rest of the animals came dragging slowly in.

The little girl and boy then had the laugh on their parents and the rest of the people for making fun of the animal they had made.

When Grandfather finished telling the story, we had much to think about. We had never paid any attention to the burro, but we decided to look at him more closely the next day.

As he left our hogan, Grandfather said, "Tomorrow, I want you to look around out there on the flat and see what birds and animals you can see. Tomorrow night, I will tell you another story about some of them. They all have their story."

Gratitude

We went to our beds of sheepskins and robes. It seemed that we had hardly fallen asleep before our mother called us to get up, saying that another day had come, the dawn was opening the curtains for the sun to come through, and we must take the ashes out from the hogan before the sun came up.

We asked her why we must always get the ashes out so early in the morning. She explained that the ashes must not blow into the sun's eyes or he could not see his way clearly. Besides, by taking them out while still dark, we could see any glowing coals and take care of them so they would not start a fire around the hogan.

After we took out the ashes and the fire was burning brightly, Mother roasted some sheep ribs over the coals, made some bread of cornmeal, and gave us our breakfast. Then she sent us out with the sheep.

The sun had not quite risen when we started the sheep out of the corral. The wind was not blowing very hard, but we knew it would come up again with the sun because it always blows three days at that time of year. We did not worry about the wind, though, as we were thinking of the burro we were riding. We could hardly wait until we could get the sheep out to feed so we would have time to look at him more closely.

About the time we got the sheep to feeding, the sun came up in a red haze, as the sand was veiling his face. The wind began to blow furiously, but it did not bother us nearly as much as it had the day before.

We looked at our burro, and sure enough, his nose and belly were white with the stardust that was left after the Milky Way was made. His hoofs were black jet, his legs were striped with bars of jet, his hair did really look like the fuzz of the cattail, and his ears were just like a jackrabbit's. We said we wished that we could see his heart, liver, and lungs. How beautiful they must be, all made with jewels.

Sandstorms are a common occurrence in the Monument Valley area, creating hazy conditions. Wolfkiller learned that early spring winds, although unpleasant, usually are over after three days.

I told my brother that I wished we would have been made of beautiful things, as the burro was. How nice it must be to be made of beautiful things inside.

We were so absorbed in studying the burro that we did not hear our grandfather when he rode up to us. He got off his horse and came to us just as I said I wished we could have been made of beautiful things inside.

"You *are* made of beautiful things inside," he said, "but you can turn all of the beautiful things to ugly, mean things if you do not try to keep them beautiful. If you allow yourselves to become angry and think evil thoughts, it will soon poison you so that you can no longer find the path of light. You will soon be like a tree that has stood in stagnant water until the insides of its roots turn black and soft. From this day on, you must try to keep your thoughts on the straight path ahead and not look for evil and feel discontented.

"Think of the burro that goes on day after day carrying you so patiently. He does not complain about the work that he has to do. Think of what I told you yesterday—of the times when our people suffered from hunger and cold day after day and year after year. Do not worry about the wind blowing. We cannot help it, and there is some reason for it.

"You know there is a Great Spirit over all, who controls everything, and what comes to us is his business—not ours. Of course, he does not want us just to sit still and not try to make things better. You know that when we pray we always say 'now all is peace' or 'now all is well' at the end of every prayer because we must believe that we will receive what we ask for. Keep your thoughts on the beautiful things you see around you. They may not seem beautiful to you at first, but if you look at them carefully, you will soon learn that everything has some beauty in it."

Just then, a desert sparrow flew out of the sagebrush nearby. "Do you see that little bird?" Grandfather asked. "Don't you think he is beautiful?"

I replied that he was just a little gray bird and not nearly as pretty as a bluebird or an oriole. Grandfather promised to tell us the story of the making of the desert sparrow when the sun had finished his work and we could again sit by the hogan fire.

He said he must now go on with the work he had to do and we must watch the sheep and get them back to the corral safely. With this, he rode away.

We went on talking about the burro and watching the sheep as they fed on the brush and weeds around us. Several sparrows were flying about. We wondered what their story would be and whether we would like it as well as we had liked the story about the burro. The sparrows still did not seem very pretty to us, but I said we might see them in a different light after hearing Grandfather's story.

The wind blew harder and harder as the day went on, but somehow we did not mind it at all. Now we had other things to think about.

Before we thought the day could possibly be nearly done, the sun was sinking far to the west in a red haze, and the shadows were lengthening toward the east. It was time to take the sheep back to the hogan, and we realized we were getting hungry. We completed our chores and were soon back home.

Our mother was roasting the meat for our supper and baking the corn bread on a hot stone by the side of the fire. We were very hungry, and the food looked so good. We ate just two meals each day, as our people think it is not right to eat too much. I had not thought much about this before, and decided to ask Mother why we believed this.

"My son," she replied, "you must be waking up like the earth awakens in the spring, when the first clap of thunder comes to call her from her winter's sleep and to tell her it is time to be up and send forth the plants for the food for her children. Have you never seen a snake when he has eaten too much—how helpless he is? He cannot even protect himself. He lies quietly and does not notice anything around him. Now a snake was made that way and must live his life as he was made to live it, but you are different. You were not made to lie dormant until you have digested your food. You would have a hard time hiding away for the time it takes you to digest it. Have you never noticed how sleepy you get if you eat too much? You do not even want to play. So, if you are greedy and always eat too much, you cannot live the life you were meant to live."

It was good to be in the hogan, out of the wind. Our home, with its pallets of sheepskins and robes and a fire in the center, seemed like a different place to me tonight. I was thinking of what Grandfather had told us about the blessings we had that we should be thankful for. Somehow, the hogan looked different, and so did our mother and sister. I thought of what Grandfather had said of the beautiful things we were made of inside, and I thought he must have told the same thing to our mother when she was a little girl, as she was always ready to do what she could for everyone. She was never angry or cross, but was always smiling and ready to give us our supper when we came home. I looked at her and noticed how black and shiny her hair looked in the firelight.

Our sister took a black pottery jug from the corner and went out to milk the goats so we could have fresh milk for our supper. I looked at the blankets in the loom, on which she and Mother had been weaving all day, and I really noticed them for the first time. I thought how hard it must be to count the threads of the warp all day and put in each colored thread of the wool so they would make the design come out right. There, by the side of the blanket, were all of the colored balls of yarn that they had washed, carded, dyed, and spun. I thought how foolish I had been when I had told my brother the day before that our mother and sister had nothing to do but sit by the hogan fire, weave blankets, and cook. The cooking must be hard, and the blanket weaving must be even harder.

Our sister came in with the goat's milk about the time that Father and Grandfather arrived. Mother said that our supper was ready, and we all sat down around the fire to eat.

Blanket weaving requires great skill. The yarn that this weaver is using appears to be handmade, probably from the wool of her own sheep, and either of natural colors or dyed using native plants. Designs, such as this, are conceived and implemented based only on a mental image. The earliest weavings were used as clothing. This one was probably intended for use as a rug.

Contentment

After we finished eating, Mother asked us to take out the bones and scraps to our dog while Father put more wood on the fire. After feeding the dog, we ran back into the hogan, for we were anxious to hear the story Grandfather had promised us.

The fire was now burning brightly. We sat down around Grandfather as the firelight played over his face and white hair. We could hear the wind blowing outside, but everything was peaceful inside the hogan and we were all contented.

Grandfather began the story he had promised to tell us, and we soon forgot everything else in the world, just listening to his voice and the low humming of the wind on the smoke hole in the top of the hogan.

The Desert Sparrow

Mr. Owl (*hastiin né'éshjaa'*) was drinking near the edge of a lake one day, and he got some of the sticky mud on his toes. He tried to get it off, but it was stuck fast. He flew away a short distance, and then the mud dropped off.

Shortly after this, the God of Poverty (*Haashch'ééh Łání*) came along and saw the mud. He looked at it and wondered what that gray, sticky stuff was and from where it could have come. "There is nothing like it here that I can see," he said to himself. Just then, he saw the lake nearby and went to its edge. There he saw the tracks of the owl and concluded that the ball of mud had come from the lake.

He sat down by the lake, took some of the mud, and started molding it in his fingers. "I will make something out of this mud," he said. "It is very nice and smooth to make things out of." He first thought he would make a snake of it. Then he said to himself, "No, I will not make a snake because snakes are horrid things, and I think there are enough snakes on the earth. I do not like snakes. They are nasty, creepy things. I will make a locust (*wóóneeshch'įįdii*)." He then started to make one, but soon changed his mind, "Locusts are very noisy

Wolfkiller's grandfather told him the story of Mr. Owl, who stepped in some sticky mud at the edge of a lake. One of the few lakes in the area was Lake Pagahrit, north of the San Juan River. It washed out in a flash flood in 1915.

and they eat so much food that other things need. There are plenty of them on the earth, so I will not make any more." He thought and thought, and then finally decided to make a bird unlike any bird that was on the earth. "I will call him desert sparrow," he said.

He molded a very small bird out of the mud. Then he looked at his creation. "My, but you are ugly," he exclaimed. "You have no feathers. I must get something to make you feathers of. What shall I use? I cannot leave you like that."

He walked around and around, looking for something to make the feathers out of. After hunting a long time, he decided he would use some of the leaves of the sagebrush to make the feathers. He gathered a few of the softest leaves and put them on the sparrow for feathers.

He then looked at his work and said, "I think you are a very presentable bird after all. You will have to live among the sage since you are so small and cannot protect yourself from the other animals that might try to catch you. Your coat is just the color of sage, so you will not be easily seen there."

The desert sparrow then looked at himself. "How ugly you have made me," he said to the God of Poverty. "Why did you make a bird at all? Could you not make a better looking bird? I know everyone will laugh at me when they see me. They will say, 'What an ugly looking thing he is—I wonder where he came from.' I will have to tell them that the God of Poverty made me out of a piece of nasty, gray, sticky mud and pasted sage leaves all over me for feathers. Then they will say, 'I thought that you were made by the God of Poverty and were made of nasty, sticky mud, and sage leaves for feathers. You look just like poverty itself.' I think it was horrid of you to make me at all if you could not make me more beautiful."

"I think you look very good, considering the things that you have been made of," the God of Poverty replied. "It all depends on yourself as to what people will think of you. If you act right, they will think you are pretty, but if you are always angry and mean, they will think that you are ugly. You can be happy and cheerful and everyone will like you, or you can be cross and mean and everyone will hate you."

"Well, now that I am made, I will do all that I can to be cheerful and pleasant to everyone," said the desert sparrow.

"That is the right way to look at life," said the God of Poverty. "Some people think that I am the worst thing in the world. I do not worry about it, though. It is worse to be untruthful or to have a bad disposition than it is to be poor. I know it is not the most pleasant thing in the world to be poor, but most people come to me of their own free will. They are either too lazy or too mean to make a good living. Of course they are sometimes sick, but if they would be cheerful about their situation, someone would help them."

"I suppose you are right," replied the desert sparrow, "and I will not complain about my coat or being made of nasty, gray, sticky mud again."

"Goodbye," said the God of Poverty. "I must be going. I hope, my son, that you will keep your good resolutions and try to make the spot where you are here among the sage a pleasant place to live."

"Goodbye, my father. I will do what I can to make it a pleasant place to live. It is not such a bad place after all, and gray is not such an ugly color. The sun shines here as well as in the meadows, the rain falls, and I can see the rainbow, the dawn, the sunset, the lightning, and the beautiful rocks just as well from here as from that pretty cottonwood over there."

"That is the way to look at life—and goodbye again," said the God of Poverty, and he went on his way.

Just then, Mr. Nighthawk (*hastiin biízhii*) came along. "Good morning, my little friend," he said. "What a beautiful coat you have."

"Thank you, my friend," said the desert sparrow. "I think my coat is rather pretty. Although it is not as pretty as your black-and-white one, I will be satisfied with it."

"I do not think my coat is half as pretty as yours," the nighthawk replied. "So you see we are never satisfied with what we have, but always want what someone else has. It is too bad we are like that, but I suppose there is a reason or we would not be so."

Just then, the wind whispered to them and said, "It is bad to be too much dissatisfied, but if we were all content to just sit down and not try to better ourselves, it would be a sad world. There would be no breeze blowing, the sun would not move, and we should all die. So you see the Creator knew best when he made us, but he did not intend that we should be unpleasant or have an ugly disposition because we are dissatisfied. He has no patience with us when we try to make things unpleasant for others, and he punishes us for our actions. We should make the best of our circumstances when we cannot change them, but there is usually a way to change the things we do not like if we try."

Vision

When another dawn came and we were eating our breakfast, Grandfather told us that he was going away for five days to perform a medicine chant for a man, but that he would tell us some more stories when he returned. He asked us to look carefully about us and try to remember what we saw so we could tell him about it when he returned.

"You know now that what I have said to you is true," he said. "All things are beautiful and full of interest if you observe them closely and study them.

"If I had not had a mother and father who were walking in the path of light, I might now be like some of the people we know who are always trying to find evil in all things. They are always scolding their children and finding fault with their lot. They are not trying to find the path of light. But we must not think of the evil in them too much, and we must try to help them if we can. If we all get our minds to working on them and wishing them well, they will soon get the light again. But, of course, they may have to have some punishment to get them into the right path. It may be the death of the more evil ones in their family. Some people will not allow themselves to be changed. The evil spirit is as solid in them as a tree is rooted to the ground. It would take much digging to get it out, and the digging must be done with the thoughts of the people around them. It is not only for the benefit of the evil ones that we want them changed. An evil thought is a thing that, when turned loose, will bring evil to all the people. We must never think or say anything we do not really want to happen. We must always think of peace ahead of us.

"I do not have time to talk anymore to you now, as I have a long ride ahead of me today. I must go and find my horse, and you must get the sheep to feed."

With this, Grandfather left the hogan and we went to the corral to take the sheep out to feed.

The sun had come from behind the curtains of the dawn with his face bright and shining, and not as he had come the day before with a red veil of sand over his face. We were glad, as we knew that the windstorm was almost over.

After we got the sheep to feeding, we began looking around us to find things to tell Grandfather about. We studied a raven that came near us. How black he looked. Then he would change to green as the sun shown on his feathers. How he glistened in the sun!

We sat quietly to wait for the sparrows to come from among the sage to fly around in the sunshine. We did so want to see all of their marks since Grandfather had told us the story about them the night before. We watched them for a while, but we could not see them very well, as they were afraid to come very near us. We lay close to the ground and were very still, but it was a long time before they came close. At last they were close enough for us to see them clearly. They really were very pretty, with their gray feathers and bright eyes. For the first time we noticed the red around their bills.

The wind was not blowing hard as it had been the two days before, but it now only came in gusts. We were glad, as it was very disagreeable to have a heavy wind blowing. We tried not to think of the wind, though, as we remembered what Grandfather had said about not thinking of things we did not want to happen and things that were somebody else's business. "We must be thankful for this day," I told my brother. We knew tomorrow would be more pleasant than today, as the windstorm was almost over.

When the windstorms pass, the days are often pleasant.

We looked at the sand dunes more closely, and what we had thought were just piles of red sand now took on for us different shapes. They were beautiful in the sunlight, covered with waves like water. They had the appearance of the rocks of the high mesas, except that they were soft. We wondered if the rocks had once been soft dunes of sand. This was the work of the wind.

We had thought the wind was just a useless thing to cause us unhappiness, but now we saw that it had many purposes. It cleared the air of the odors of decaying plants and dead animals, brought the clouds on its wings to give us rain, and made us strong.

The day seemed to go very fast, and it was nearly sunset before we felt tired or hungry. It was time to take the sheep in to get them settled for the night. As we drove them across the flat toward the water hole, we saw the sun setting in a beautiful bank of bright yellow and red clouds. "We will ask Mother about the sun tonight," I said. "We will ask her to tell us where he goes at night."

When the sheep were in the corral and our supper was over, we sat around the hogan fire. Father came in and told us that black clouds were rising very fast. Just then, we heard a low rumble of thunder. Father and Mother stood up and stretched themselves. They told us we must do the same. We did as they said, and so did our sister. When we sat down again, we asked Father why we must do this.

"Earth, our mother, is now awake," he said. "She is stretching as one stretches after a long night's sleep. All through the winter, she has rested. Now she is going to send out plants for her children. Soon the earth will be covered with grass and flowers, and the trees will be green again."

I thought of what Grandfather had said about everything being beautiful and having a purpose. How foolish I had been all my life not to notice the things around me.

Faith

That evening my brother and I told our mother about the sunset we had seen—yellow and red clouds with the bright streaks of light coming down to meet the red rock of the mesa and dipping down over the canyon walls. We asked her where the sun went at night.

"The sun goes back to his wife in the west when his day's work is done," she answered. "Far to the west of us is a Great Water, and one wife of the sun lives in it. This woman is called the Changing Woman because she can change herself from old to young at will."

"Have you ever seen the Great Water?" I asked.

"No, my children, I have never seen it," she answered. "But our people have gone there from time to time to get foam, water, and shells for some of our ceremonies. They have told us about the Great Water. It is so wide you could not see across it if you could keep sending your eyes ahead of you, as you would send an arrow from your bow."

"But how did our people know this Great Water was there?" I asked.

"Well, my son," she answered, "I will tell you the clan story that has been told to our children for many generations. All of us must remember it and tell it to our children as soon as they are old enough to understand. I would have waited for two or three years yet to tell it to you, for I am afraid you are too young to remember how it goes for very long. But I can tell it to you now, and if you forget the details you can ask me to tell it to you again when you are older."

Origin of the People

Our people once lived in a land of darkness. What I mean is they knew nothing about the things around them, so it was as if they were living in the darkness of night. They had not yet found the spirit of speech and were like animals. Since they were unable to talk to each other very much, each one went his or her own way, looking for food and not caring what the others did.

Wolfkiller's mother told him that some of the people had gone to the Great Water (the Pacific Ocean) to gather foam, water, and shells for their ceremonies. This appears to be Hoskinnini Begay on the left and Wolfkiller on the right reenacting an ancient pilgrimage.

Eventually the people came up a little higher and moved to a place that was better, although the soil there was very poor and the water was salty. They still were not very intelligent, but they continued to learn as the years went by.

Their next move was to a beautiful land called Mountain Slope (*nábinibidii,* "a slope near the summit"),where trees and flowers grew and many kinds of food were available. There they lived happily for many years. This place was across the Great Water, and it is where they learned to plant corn, weave, and make pottery.

In their new home were many beautiful seashells—enough for everyone to have all they wanted. The people wore no ornaments and dressed only in the skins of animals. These were their only possessions. All the people shared the land, and they had no disagreements about where they should gather seeds and fruits. They shared the corn, too, and all helped plant it.

The people thought they were safe from trouble, but trouble eventually came to them. The chief of the people, White Light of the Heavens (*Yoołgai,* "White Shell"), was married to the beautiful Spirit Woman.[1] She was a member of the Spirit Clan, a group that was very impulsive, like the spirits of the wind, rain, and lightning. Spirit Woman was like them, coming and going whenever she wanted. White Light loved her very much and tried to make her happy, but he could not control her as he did the other people.

The People of Darkness—those who had stayed behind—began to visit Mountain Slope and soon learned that it was a pleasant place to live. Spirit Woman spent most of her time visiting and dancing with them, and she fell in love with their leader, Coyote of the Dark Land (*Yá'ąąsh Mą'ii,* "Coyote of the Land Beyond the Sky"). He was handsome, a great warrior, and a thief, as the coyote are now.

This man began to make raids on the people of Mountain Slope. White Light thought this would turn his wife against the People of Darkness, but it had the opposite effect. She admired them for their spirit. "You are truly like the spirits of the wind, rain, and lightning," she told them.

Soon Spirit Woman persuaded the People of Darkness to move to Mountain Slope. This was not hard to do, as Coyote was as much in

1 To Wolfkiller, the brilliance of the predawn sky was like the inside of a white seashell.

love with her as she was with him. White Light was opposed to this, but at last his wife persuaded him to let them stay.

White Light said they could move there only if they agreed to come under his rule, stop their raids, and do their part of the work. The People of Darkness consented and came to live at Mountain Slope.

Everything went well for a short time, but soon Coyote and Spirit Woman began to lead the people astray. They cared for nothing but pleasure and spent all of their time going around from one place to another, singing and dancing. The women all admired Spirit Woman and were ready to follow her. Things went from bad to worse. The women would not weave or make pottery anymore, and they stopped taking care of their children.

Coyote and Spirit Woman began to meet in secret. Soon one of the wives of Coyote found out about these meetings and told the chief what she knew.

White Light was very angry and called a council to tell the men that they must leave the beautiful land. He said that the spirit of unrest would soon cause the people to go back to the dark stage since they no longer had any interest in the things about them. They were all thinking evil thoughts and wishing they could kill someone.

"There is a land toward the rising sun," White Light said. "Tomorrow, we will start to build rafts as we will have to go out on the water. We will take every man and boy from the land—even little babies. After we have gone, the women may see the light and try to do better. We must not tell the women what we have decided here until we are ready to start. From then on, they can dance and play as much as they care to, as there will be no one to disturb them."

The men ordered Coyote to join them, threatening to kill him if he did not cooperate. With all of his bravado, he was secretly afraid of the chief, so he relented.

When the men completed building the rafts, and the food and seeds were ready, White Light called all of the people together and told the women what they were going to do. Some of the women cried and said they wanted to go, too, but Spirit Woman said she was glad to be rid of the men.

The men embarked for the land across the Great Water. They took all of the men and boys, and even one baby who had been born the night before. It took them four days to cross the water.

As soon as they left, the women began to dance and rejoice, led by Spirit Woman. They continued this for a time, but soon they found that they would have to do something to get food. They tried to hunt and till the soil, but were unsuccessful and became more and more impoverished. From time to time, some of them tried to make rafts with which to cross the water, but they were unable to make them strong enough to hold together in the waves.

White Light still loved Spirit Woman, and he hoped and prayed that she would see the light. He occasionally sent some spies to see how the women were getting along.

After four years, the spies reported that they had heard Spirit Woman praying to the Great Water to send White Light to her. He was very happy and at once sent a number of rafts to bring the women across the water. This is what White Light had waited for so long. There was great rejoicing and feasting in the new land when the women arrived. They found a beautiful land on this side of the Great Water—even more beautiful than the land from which they had come. There were many trees, flowers, grasses, and streams, and beautiful birds, deer, and antelope.

For a time the people were happy and contented. Coyote was still in their midst, however, and he was still a great thief. One day he saw the baby of the Water Spirit, which is an animal who is able to control the water. Coyote decided to steal the baby (a small sea animal) and cover up his tracks so no one would be able to tell who had taken it. After a few days, a great storm and a great flood came from the big water. The people saw a white light rising toward them. They went to the top of a nearby hill and saw that it was a great flood, with spray that reached high into the sky. They climbed higher and higher until they came to the top of a big mountain. Still, the water came to surround them. It was cold on the mountain, but they could not go down, as there was water all around them.

White Light called all of the people together. He found that many had been lost in the flood. He asked them who had committed the great sin that had caused the waters to come against them. No one answered. Then he asked them again, but still no one answered. He asked them a third time, but got no answer that time either. Then he looked into the faces about him and saw the guilt on the face of Coyote. "I see guilt in the eyes of the chief of the People of Darkness," he said. "You have caused great trouble with your evil thoughts. What have you done this time?"

Then all of the people were angry at Coyote. Even some of the more advanced of his own people were angry with him and said he must die. He became frightened, took the baby from the bag in which he was carrying it, and threw it back into the water. Then the water began to recede from the people.

"As soon as we can get around again, you and your people must leave us," White Light ordered Coyote.

After a few days, when the water had gone down enough so they could get around again, the People of Darkness left the people of Mountain Slope. However, from that time to this day our people have not had such great peace as they had before Coyote and his evil thoughts came among them.

For many years after this, the people were happy and contented. The trees and plants grew again, and the work of life went on. There was much food and many beautiful birds and plants from which to make clothes. There were many deer, antelope, and all kinds of other animals.

Then the young men became discontented again. They grew tired of the efforts of gathering food and the cotton fiber and feathers of birds from which to make their clothes. They started to gamble. They gambled day and night when the moon was light, but when the moon was dark, they would rest, for they were too lazy to gather wood for firelight.

The old people told the young men that they must work to live, but nothing they said did any good. Just then, when things were at their worst, when there was no food laid by from the abundance that was everywhere, the rain stopped coming and all of the plants dried up and the trees did not bloom. The people caught fish from the Great Water, gathered a few berries, and dug roots to live on. Still the rain did not come, and soon all of the plants were gone and there was nothing left but the fish. The people grew weaker, and many of them died.

As the water dried up, the springs grew weaker and the streams stopped running. Day after day, it grew hotter and hotter. Soon the animals and birds started moving to higher land—toward the dawn. The people followed them. Then came a time when the wind ceased to blow. Not even a breath was stirring. The birds could not fly, and the deer, antelope, and other animals died of thirst and hunger. Still the people went on, trying to find a land where they could get enough food to keep life in their bodies.

Our group came to a place at the base of a big rock where a spring was still living. At this place, they saw four deer drinking. That is why our clan is called the Deer Spring Clan. A few plants were still growing there. There the people lived for a short time, but then the spring died. Some of the strong men were sent out to see if anything else was living on the earth. By this time, the plants were all gone. There were still a few rats and mice, and the people had to live on those.

When the scouts returned, they told the people that there was still some water to the east, and a few plants, deer, and antelope were still alive there. So the people moved on across a land that was just white-hot sand. Those who were still alive were just bones and dry, parched skin. Their hair was matted and dead. As the days went by, some of them became too weak to continue, and they stopped by the trail and died. Day after day, this went on. Still the rain did not come and the earth grew hotter, with not a breath of air stirring.

When the survivors reached the high mountains, they found the plants as the men had told them. By this time, only four of our clan people were left—two men and two women. Some of the people of other clans came to the same place. None of them could think of anything but food.

The rain had not fallen for twelve winters. The people decided it was time to pray. Then the wind came again, and on its wings, the soft, black clouds came out of the Great Water, our mother. Then they knew they would live again. Soon the land was beautiful and the people were happy again. They resolved to keep up the ceremonies and pray for help when they needed it.

For many years, everything went well. Then the people became dissatisfied again. They became tired of just doing the same thing year after year, so they began to make raids on the people who lived around them. Soon they were too lazy to plant their own fields. They would wait until other people tilled the fields and harvested their crops, and then they went in numbers and made war on these people and took their corn from them. They again broke their promise to the Great Spirit. Once again, evil thoughts filled the land.

The people had trouble among themselves. Some of them left the land where they had been living and came to the land where we now are. Our people again had peace for a time. However, we now have more enemies, as the people who did not come here have made war on us from time to time.

When the story was finished, I lay awake on my sheepskin bed and thought of the hardships our people had gone through on the way to this land where we now lived. How much more beautiful this land must be than some of the places Mother told us about. How thankful we should be for what we now had.

When the dawn came, the world seemed different. I looked over the mountains far to the east and saw the white light above them. Never before had the sky looked white and glistening as it looked that morning—like the inside of a shell, all bright and beautiful. Then, as the sun came over the horizon, the mountains turned to red and yellow, and then to blue. It was beautiful! Why had I never seen it before?

Resolve

Each night, when we returned to our hogan, we looked for our grandfather, but he was not there. After twelve days, he finally returned. We were so glad to see him, as we were anxious to hear some more of his stories.

He explained that while he was performing the ceremony, another man came and asked him to perform a ceremony for his mother. That is where he had gone after the first ceremony was over.

While he was at the second place, some men came in with disturbing news from the east. Some of the young men of our people had just returned from a trip they had made east of the Rio Grande. They had made a raid on the people of the villages and had brought back some girls and sheep.

Grandfather said he had hoped that the spirit of peace had come to live forever in our land, as, for the past several years, the people had seemed contented. But now it appeared that the spirit of war was returning. He blamed the young men for this.

The young men were blamed for rekindling the spirit of war.

"We have plenty of food now, and it is not as it was some years ago," he said. "There has been rain to make our corn grow, and we have sheep to give us meat and goats to give us milk. We do not need the new blood that the girls would bring into our tribe. In years gone by, we were compelled to go out and steal girls to save the life of our people, as there were so few of us and we could not marry into our own families. But now we have many clans."

I asked him what he meant by saying that at one time we were compelled to steal girls. He said he would tell us of the raids on the other tribes some other time, as he did not have time to talk about it that night. The older people wanted to hear more of the news of the day.

He said that some of the young men had gone on what the old people thought was to be a trading trip. They said that they wanted to take some blankets and buckskins to trade for beads and turquoise. The women wove many blankets for them to trade. When the young men returned, they came with girls and sheep. They had traded the blankets and buckskins for beads and turquoise, and the Pueblo people thought they were friendly. They treated them as friends, but then they did this terrible thing. Now, because of their evil thoughts, some of our people would have to suffer.

The old people were afraid of what would happen. I saw sadness come into the faces around the fire and thought how foolish I had been to wish to become a raider and cause all of the light to go out of the lives of all the people. I thought of what Grandfather had told us about a thought being a thing that would bring either good or evil, and I wondered if my foolish talk would cause any of the trouble that our people feared would come.

Grandfather talked far into the night to our family. He told us of the times gone by when we had war year after year. Some of these times our people were to blame, but most of the time it had been the other tribes who had made the raids on us to take the food we had worked so hard for. He said that the people of the villages had never made war on us, although they had cause to do so. "They are a peaceful people, and we had hoped they would be our friends for all time, but now we have again caused the thought of war to go forth in the land."

One of the other elders of the family then spoke. "We must try to stop the evil spirit before it becomes like a great storm that would cause the people to go down, as the rocks and trees go down before a great flood.

We must not let ourselves think that that will happen. We must not fear. We must work and pray as we have in the past that this evil may go from us. We must try to turn the minds of the people into the path of light. We must plant corn and gather all of the foods that grow around us. We must keep the minds of the people from the dark path of war. Much work will help them think of other things."

We went to our beds and tried to sleep, but I could not get rid of the thought that I had helped to bring this evil on my people. I fell into a troubled sleep, and my dreams were of war. I was glad when the dawn came.

I told my family of my dreams. They said we must have a ceremony to dispel the evil dreams. My father also had dreamed of war. In his dream, many of our people were hiding in a high-walled canyon, and warriors came into the land. "We must not talk of these dreams," he said. "We must get our minds off such things."

I asked my mother if she thought I had helped to bring this trouble on our people by my evil thoughts and my talk when I said that I wished we could go back to the time when all I would have to do was to steal girls from the Pueblos and fight the Utes and Apaches.

She answered that the evil thought of even the youngest would have its effect, but she did not believe that I was the one who had started this thing. "The young men who went out on the trading trip were probably the ones who first had the thought of war," she said. "But even the least among us who sends forth evil thoughts can cause us much trouble, just as a trail of one horse going over the sand can cause the water from a heavy storm to make a deep wash. The water runs down through the tracks, and from the depression there is a place for the water to run the next time the rain falls. The more one travels over these trails, the deeper the wash gets. We must not talk or think anymore about our fears than we can help. Go out, my son, and take care of the sheep. Try to see the good about you. It may seem best to the Great Spirit for us to have a little trouble now, as many of the people are drifting away from the path they know they should follow. Let us not help to spread the clouds of evil over our lands by adding our thoughts to the rest."

Our neighbors began preparing to have a medicine man come to our hogan the next night to say some prayers and dispel the effects of the bad dreams my father and I were having. We knew they would no longer speak of their fears, so we hoped Grandfather would tell us another story.

Desire

That evening, after we completed our work and returned to our hogan, Grandfather said he would tell us a story. "What have you seen while I was gone, and which animal or bird would you like to hear about?" he asked. We told him about the raven and asked him to tell us its story. The fire was burning brightly as Grandfather spoke.

The Raven

Many years ago, on a very beautiful day in midsummer, the sun was shining on the high peaks, the flowers were all in bloom, and the birds were out singing and having a good time—all except Mr. Raven (*hastiin gáagii*), who was very sad. He was sad because he did not have a beautiful coat like the rest of the birds. His coat was ugly, rusty, and gray.

He passed Mr. Blackbird (*hastiin ch'agii*), whose coat was black and glossy. With the sun shining on it, it looked green, gold, and black at the same time. Poor old raven said to himself, "How beautiful his coat is. I wish my coat was beautiful like that." He stopped and stared at the blackbird's beautiful glossy black coat, and then looked at his own and thought how ugly it was.

"Mr. Blackbird, what a beautiful coat you have—so glossy and black," he said. "And now, when the sun is shining on it, it looks like a rainbow. Yet when you are in the shade it is so black that you can hide if you care to. Will you give it to me?"

"No, indeed, I will not give you my coat," the blackbird replied.

The raven asked him again, but he still refused. He then said, "Please, Mr. Blackbird, my father, give me your coat."

He again refused him, but feeling sorry for him said, "Why do you care whether your coat is beautiful or not? Don't you know, my son, that the main thing in life is to be beautiful inside? Maybe your heart is made of beautiful jewels. Don't you know that it is not the most beautiful flowers and trees that give us food? Just look over there at the jimson weed (*ch'óhejilyééh*) at the foot of that rock. See how beautiful his blossoms and leaves are, and yet he is full of sin. If we should eat his roots, we would soon be crazy and lose our eyes. Then there is the loco weed (*náá'ádin*). It is also beautiful with its wonderful purple blossoms, but he is full of sin. We even call him "no eyes" because he takes our eyes. On the other hand, there are the different grasses. They are not nearly as beautiful as these other plants. They have no beautiful blossoms of purple, lavender, or white, yet from them we get our life, our food."

"That is all true, my father," the raven replied. "Still I would like to have a beautiful coat like yours. You are not sinful just because you have a beautiful coat, and you must be very wise to know all of the things you have told me. Could I not have a beautiful coat like yours, which looks like the rainbow? The rainbow is not sinful, is it? It comes to tell us when the rain is falling to make the trees, flowers, and grass grow. Then there is the sun. It is beautiful. So also are the water, the mountains, and trees. Look at that red bluff over there. Is it not beautiful with the sun shining on it? It looks as if it was burning, and at other times, when the shadows of evening fall upon it, it looks purple."

The blackbird thought a moment and then said, "You can make your coat black like mine with the soot from the chimney."

"Mr. Blackbird, my father, I do not believe that your coat is made black with the soot from the chimney," said the raven.

"You are right, my son," replied the blackbird. "It is not soot, but a yellow stone and pitch that make a beautiful black dye."

The raven then said, "Hi-he," which in bird language is, "I believe that," and he began to laugh and laugh to think what a beautiful black coat he could have had all these years had he known what the blackbird had known all this time. He laughed and laughed, holding his sides and rolling over and over until he lost his breath. He tried to catch it, but he could not stop laughing. Then he fainted.

The blackbird was very badly frightened, and he flew away to get some pinyon gum. He quickly found some and flew back to where the raven lay in a faint. Then he quickly gathered some coals, put the pinyon gum on them, and held them under the raven's nose so he would breathe the smoke. He also put some of

Besides providing shade and wood, trees are a source of sticky gum that is used as glue.

the melted gum on the raven's beak. It ran down the sides of his nose and made whiskers.

The blackbird had to laugh because the raven looked so funny. Then he said to himself, "This will never do. I will have to smooth down his beak and make it a nice shape, even though it is large. So he worked and worked until he had molded the beak into a very pretty shape. Even today, ravens have a large beak and whiskers.

The smoke from the pinyon gum brought the raven to. He got to his feet and said, "Thank you very much, my father."

"Go to that clear pool of water and see what you think of your beautiful beak and whiskers," the blackbird said.

The raven flew to the pool and looked into the water. When he saw himself, he was so surprised that he nearly fainted again. He did not look like himself with the large beak and whiskers. He sat down under the shade of a tree and gazed at his image in the water. He did not know whether he liked the change or not. At last, he decided that he did like it. He told the blackbird that he liked the large beak and whiskers, "as it makes me look much more distinguished. If I had a beautiful coat like yours, I would look fine."

The blackbird saw that it was no use trying to change the raven's mind about his coat, so he took the coat that was all gray and rust, made some dye of the yellow stone and pitch, and put the coat in it. It came out very black and glossy. He then hung it on the limb of a tree to dry. When it was dry, he put some of the pinyon gum on the shoulders so the raven would always have some of the medicine with him if he fainted again. That is what makes the ugly burned-looking places on the raven's wings.

The blackbird did not tell the raven the truth when he said that he dyed his own coat with yellow stone and pitch. His pretty black coat never fades, but the raven's coat gets brown spots from the sun in the summertime.

The blackbird had also put some pitch on the raven's feet after he had revived from his faint, so he might get entirely well. He became so engrossed in dying the raven's coat that he forgot about the pitch. When he realized his oversight, the sun was already down. "We must go to bed now, my son," he told the raven. "Tomorrow, I will make your feet smooth." The next morning, just as the first streak of dawn came, the blackbird went to the raven and said, "Come, my son, and let me take the rough pitch off your feet." However, when he tried to get it off, it would not come because it had gotten hard during the night. So today the raven's feet are all rough from the pinyon gum that the blackbird put on them.

The story took the people's minds off their fears. We all went to bed, thinking of what we had heard.

The next day my brother and I went out with our work of herding. We had something else to think of besides our fears. We studied the raven and talked about the things our grandfather had told us about him. What was the reason people could not be satisfied with their lot in life, we wondered. But this is none of our business. We were made that way, so there must be a reason for it.

Hope

The afternoon was bright and beautiful, but the air was still quite cold. We started the sheep for the hogan just as the sun was dropping toward the red mesas in the west. When we reached our hogan, we saw many horses around it. All of the people from the country around us had come to take part in the ceremonies that the medicine man was performing that night.

Father had taken his sweat bath and washed his hair, and he was ready for the prayers that were to be said for him. Mother, our father's sister, and some of the other women of the family were baking corn bread and roasting meat for the people who had come to take part in the ceremonies. Men and women were sitting all around the hogan, talking of the things they had been doing. They did not say anything about their fears of war. When the food was ready, we all gathered in the hogan and ate our meal.

A gathering at an exceptionally large hogan. This type of hogan is made of logs laid horizontally.

When we were finished eating, the medicine man came in and took his place on the west side. The men arranged themselves in their places on the west and south sides, and the women sat down on the north side and up to the door toward the east. When all was ready, the medicine man began to chant, and all of the men joined in. I sat with my father, as the people said I must take part in the ceremony since I also had had bad dreams. When the chants were finished, the medicine man asked my father and me to sit in front of him. He told me that I must be very careful not to make a mistake, as it would spoil the effect of the prayer if I did, and it would cause me trouble. I listened with all my might to his words.

After the prayer, the medicine man told me the story of the first time the prayer was used.

> Many years ago, a little girl was very sick from a bad dream she had had. She could not eat, could not sleep at night, and lay on her bed for many days. One day the wind came to her and said, 'It is the Bear that makes you sick. You must get the bear singer to sing for you.'
>
> The girl's people went to the bear singer and asked him to come and sing for her. However, before he could go, he had to ask the Bear—the Blue Bear, the White Bear, the Yellow Bear, and the Black Bear.[2]
>
> The Bear asked the bear singer, 'What will the Navajo give us for the use of our medicine?'
>
> The Navajo replied, 'We will give the Black Bear a jet basket, the Blue Bear a turquoise basket, the Yellow Bear a pearl basket, and the White Bear a white shell basket.'
>
> 'It is well,' the Bear said to the bear singer. 'Go and sing for the child. But it will take you four days to cure her.'
>
> The bear singer went. The first day he sang she improved a little. The next day she was much better. The third day she was nearly well, and the fourth day she was as well as ever.
>
> Before he left, the bear singer said, 'Now I will teach you how to sing for those who are sick, by the medicine of the Bear, since we are all going away in the mountain and you cannot find us anymore. So that you won't forget what I tell you of our healing, you must write the story in colored sands that you may be able to teach

2 The Bear in this story is a deity, who embodies four beings whose colors match those of the four sacred compass directions.

one another.' He taught them how to write the story in the sand and make the pictures of the different plants—the serviceberry and the moss on the water—that are used to drive out the evil spirit of the Bear. He taught them their songs and prayers. He and the Bear then went into the mountains where they now are.

My grandson, I must tell you what we mean by praying and using the name of a bear in our prayers. The bear was a man, and not really a bear. But he had power to frighten people so they thought too much about him and would dream of awful things. The little girl in the story was frightened one day, and she let her fright work on her mind until she was very ill. That is the reason we use the bear as the symbol of fear from that day until now.

Fear is just a part of the evil spirit in us, as hate, anger, and envy are parts of this same evil spirit or evil thought. To live the right life, we must live within ourselves. Our thoughts are our own. It is ourselves that we must control.

After the ceremony was over, everyone went to bed. The hogan was full of people sleeping in their robes.

The next morning, after we ate breakfast, our visitors left for their own hogans and the day began for my brother and me. As we herded the sheep out to feed, we talked about the ceremony. We discussed whether the prayers of the medicine man would cause the war, which our people feared, to go around us.

Grandfather overheard us as he rode up on his horse. "You must believe that our prayers will be answered," he said. "Did not the medicine man say four times in his prayer that the evil has missed me? He said this four times because we do not want any evil thought to strike us either from before us, from behind us, from beneath us, or from above us. And I say to you, forget these evil thoughts and think of the other things you see around you. There are many pleasant things. Look down under your feet—the grass is beginning to come. Soon the land will be green again and there will be many more birds and animals for you to study."

I asked Grandfather how a plant could come back after it had died. "A plant does not die," he answered. "A plant grows and blossoms and puts forth seeds, and then the wind comes and carries the seeds over the earth. The dried plant goes back into the earth and gives life to the roots of the new growth. When the summer comes, the plant will be stronger for the death of the leaves unless some disease comes to kill it. A disease can kill the old plant, but since the seeds it has sent out still live, the plant is not dead.

"A disease in a plant is like evil thought in a man. If the plant has not the strength to overcome the disease, it must die. The years of our lives are as the leaves of the plant. They make us strong if our thoughts are right, but if our thoughts are evil, the years make us weaker. This body

Young shepherds have time to observe nature and contemplate life.

in which I am moving is as if it were only borrowed. It is the spirit within that lives, and when the body dies, the spirit goes out to make another start."

"Grandfather, what do you mean when you say the spirit will make another start? Does the spirit still live on after the body is dead?"

"Yes, my grandson. The spirit goes from the body to a better land than this. It is better because it is always summer there, and everyone is happy if he wants to be. Now you have your work to do and I must be going. Tonight I will tell you what you want to know."

We had much to think about all through the day, and it did not seem very long before the sun was dipping into the west again. We were looking forward to the night when our grandfather would tell us about where the spirit goes.

The evening was peaceful. We all settled in for the night and were sitting around the hogan fire. The fire sent out a soft light, as it was warmer now and we did not need much heat. Grandfather came to tell us what we wanted to know. He said that we must listen very carefully to what he was going to say, as it was very necessary that we should know that the short life we were now living was not all we were created for.

"As I told you today, nothing ever dies, and everything has a spirit that lives on forever. Even our bodies, which have been loaned to us for the time we are here, go back into our mother, the earth. After the spirit leaves, the life goes out of the body—but you know this already. The spirit goes back to the place from where it came. Even the beads and jewels and the clothing we wear go back. By this we mean the thought that has been put into the making of the things we wear goes back to the place from where it came. The thought comes from the Great Spirit and is therefore a thing to be treasured. We are nothing by ourselves. When one of us says he can live alone, it is the evil one in him who is speaking."

"Grandfather, why do we have the evil in us?" I asked.

"My grandson, we must have the evil in us to make us strong. If we did not have the evil, we would never have gained the strength that we have now. We must have the evil so that we will fight. A struggle always gives us more strength, and the harder we fight, the more we gain in strength. The ones among us who are too lazy to fight never get anything. At times, we are all tempted to sit and wait for what might come, but it is not right to do nothing. Everything is made to fight its way through life. We must work to live, and this life is not all there is, as I have told you before. If we can control ourselves, we can do anything we set out to do. Day after day we must work to gain strength to go on until the time comes when we will go out of this body.

"We do not know what we will be after we are dead, but we believe that when we go to what we call the Peaceful Land, we will find our friends there. We believe that if we live the right kind of a life here, we will be happy with our friends. When we lay this borrowed body in the lap of the Mother Earth, she knows we have no further use for it, so she receives it back. The life of the spirit goes back into the earth, too, but it goes to another land beneath the land we see while we are living here. It is more beautiful than this land, as I have told you before. And then we will have a chance to lead peaceful lives if we carry the right thoughts there with us.

"That is why, when one of us dies and goes back, he must always be dressed in new clothes and jewels. If we go dressed well, when our friends see us coming they will say, 'Here comes our friend. He must have led his life helping people. Otherwise he could not have come to us as well dressed as he is.' But if we go dressed in rags, they will say, 'Here comes that man who lived near us. He must have been a very bad man. He must have gambled away all of his goods or have done something else that was not right. His people would not have sent him to us looking as he does if he had led the right kind of a life.' So they will not greet him with a handshake or tell him that they are glad to see him."

"Grandfather," I asked, "why should death be a sad thing, as we will be much happier after we are gone from this land?"

"It is sadness for the ones who are left here, but we must try to think of the ones who are gone, just as we think of the plants when they die in the fall. We must think of the strength that the spirit has gained to do something greater in the other world. You know, my grandson, we think we will go on advancing after we go out of this body."

"It is getting late now," said Grandfather, "so we must go to sleep. I cannot talk anymore tonight."

The next day went very fast. We thought and talked of the things that Grandfather had said. Sometimes we would forget and start to think about our fears, but we tried to concentrate on the things around us as our grandfather had told us to do. With a little effort, we soon forgot the evil thought. By the time the sun was low in the west, we were happy and anxious to hear what else Grandfather had to teach us.

Nurture

When the dark came and the stars were shining brightly, Grandfather said, "Tonight I will show you the Seed Basket in the heavens and tell you how we know when it is almost time to plant our corn again." He took us out and showed us the circle of stars that the people called the Seed Basket. It was just coming up over the mountains to the east of us. He said that it soon would come up much earlier, and when it came into the heavens just after sunset, we would know that it was time to start to plant the corn.

Grandfather said that in years gone by, the people had not known anything about the stars and they planted the corn at all times. Many times they lost all of their work, as the frost came and killed the plants when they started to grow. Other times they planted so late in the spring that the corn would not ripen before the cold weather arrived again. Then an old man told them about the Seed Basket. He said they should plant their corn when the basket came into the heavens just after the sun had gone home for the night, and they would not have anymore trouble from lack of food.

Grandfather showed us many more stars in the heavens. He said they all had stories that he would tell us about sometime. We returned to the hogan and went to bed early. We had to get our rest so we would have strength for the work ahead—planting of the fields.

Our rest was peaceful that night. All of the evil thoughts had gone from our minds. We were looking forward to seeing the land green again and the flowers in bloom. I fell asleep with pleasant thoughts of the bright stars I had seen in the clear heavens, and I dreamed of a beautiful land with flowers of many different colors—white, red, blue, and yellow. How beautiful they looked against the red rocks of the mesas.

When the dawn came again and the day's work had to begin, I did not feel tired as I had when my dreams were not pleasant. I felt as if I had gotten some strength from the bright stars.

The days went by very quickly, as the people were getting the fields in shape to plant. I did not get a chance to talk much to Grandfather about the things I wanted to know. I knew, though, that when the corn was planted, we could get him to tell us some more stories about the things around us.

One evening Grandfather came into the hogan just after the sun had gone home for the night. He said the Seed Basket was in the heavens. We went outside with him and saw a circle of bright stars just coming over the mountains. It was beautiful!

"We must start to plant our corn tomorrow," he said. We went to bed early so that we would all be rested for the next day's work.

The next morning we were all up early. The men got the seed corn and started for the fields. My brother and I took the sheep out to feed as we had so many times before. Many more birds were flying around now that spring was here. We talked about the birds and other things we saw about us. We were anxious for the time when our grandfather and mother would have more time and would not feel too tired to tell us some more stories.

As the day went on, we talked about the planting of the corn. I wondered how the people knew a hard kernel of corn would make a plant. That evening, after we finished eating our supper and were resting around the fire, we asked Grandfather to explain about how the corn plant grew.

He asked me to bring him a kernel of corn. He broke it open and showed me the little white line inside of it. He explained that when planted, the kernel swells and the plant comes forth from the center of the seed. Then he took a pinyon nut and showed us the inside of it. If we planted one of them, a tree would grow from it, he said.

"Tomorrow, I want you to take some corn out to the field and plant it in a sheltered place so you will not have to plant it very deep. You can water it every day. Then you can watch it and see how the green plant comes from the seed."

I went to bed thinking of what he had said. I was glad when the morning came, as I was anxious to get the seeds in the ground.

Grandfather took us to the field and showed us where to plant the seeds. We planted and watered them before we took the sheep to feed. Every morning after this, we went by the cornfield to water the seeds and look at them. A few days went by before the seeds began to swell. Then one morning we saw little white plants coming out of some of them. As the days went by, they grew to strong green plants. We were very much interested in watching them grow.

Wolfkiller's grandfather used the nature of corn plants as an object lesson to demonstrate how moral development takes place.

When they had grown strong, Grandfather told us to bring some of the water from a spring out in the flats when we came home with the sheep that night.

"But Grandfather, the water from that spring is not good," I protested. "Why do you want it? It is very bitter."

"I know that, my grandson, but I want you to bring some of it anyway. I will tell you what I want it for tomorrow."

We talked all day about the bitter water and wondered what he would do with it. That evening, we brought the water and set it down in the corner of the hogan. We did not ask Grandfather anymore about what he wanted it for—we knew he would tell us soon.

The next morning, when we started to take the sheep out of the corral, Grandfather came to see us. He asked us to get the bitter water and, in another jug, some good water. We took both jugs out to the cornfield. Grandfather chose some of our strong plants and told us to water them with the bitter water and the other plants with the good water.

For several days, we brought the bitter water home and watered the same plants with it. Soon they began to turn yellow. We told Grandfather they were dying. "So they are, my grandson. Tonight I will tell you why I have done this. Take the sheep to feed now. I must hoe my corn to keep the weeds from killing it." We were very anxious for the night to come so we could hear what Grandfather would tell us.

That evening, after supper was over, he called us to him and said, "Now I will tell you what the bitter water was for. I wanted you to see how it would kill the plants. The bitter water is to the plants as evil thoughts are to a man. Did you notice that the plants turned paler and paler until now they are almost as white as when they came from the seeds? The care you have given them is almost for nothing. In the same way, if we allow evil thoughts to grow in us, all of our years will be lost. Tomorrow, you must start to give the plants good water again and watch them get green, but they can never be as strong as if they had never had the bitter water.

"So it is with us. If we never allow the evil thoughts to come into us, we will be much stronger. We all have the evil in us, as I have told you before, but we must fight it to keep it from controlling us. This fight makes us strong, and, as I have said before, we must fight to live. We must not let the evil spirit get control of us. If we do, we are lost just as the corn plants would be lost if you kept giving them bitter water."

The next morning we began to water the plants with good water. In a few days, they began to get green again.

Ambition

As the days went by, the corn grew greener and greener. Then the summer rains came and the cornfields looked beautiful. All of the people were happy and at peace. The grass grew and the sheep were fat. The flowers were in bloom. They looked more beautiful to me this year than they ever had before. We could take more time studying the things about us now, as the sheep rested in the shade of the rocks through the hottest part of the day. They could get all they wanted to eat in a few hours since there was so much feed for them.

One day I was sitting with my brother under the shade of a rock. We were talking about the plants and birds when I noticed a plant that was covered with blue flowers. It was beautiful, but people would not notice it if they were just riding by. "This is a beautiful plant, though the blossoms are so small," I said. "I am going to take some of it to the hogan tonight and ask Grandfather about it."

That evening, after we put the sheep into the corral and returned to the hogan, I showed the plant to him and asked him if he would tell us about it. He looked at it and said that even though it was small and grew flat to the ground and out of sight, it was important for food and medicine. When the people were hungry and the rain did not fall to make the corn grow, the people were compelled to learn what plants they could eat. That is when they learned about this plant.

"There is a story about it, and I will tell it to you now if you would like to hear it," said Grandfather.

I told him that I was so glad he was going to tell us another story because there were still so many things I wanted to learn about.

The Plant with the Blue Flowers

Dragonfly (*tániil'áí*) was flying around one day, hunting water, when the Spirit of Hunger came to him and frightened him. The dragonfly fainted. When he came to, he saw an awful thing in front of him. It was so thin that it was just a lot of bones with wings. Its eyes were very large, as there was no face for them to rest in. "I wonder what he is," thought the dragonfly.

Then the Spirit of Hunger shook his head from side to side.

The dragonfly became worried. "He can catch my thoughts without my speaking them. I wonder how he does it."

Again, the Spirit of Hunger shook his head.

"I wonder if he is the Spirit of Death," the dragonfly thought.

Again, the Spirit of Hunger shook his head.

"He must be the Spirit of Hunger," the dragonfly concluded. "He is so thin—just a spine and some eyes and wings."

Then the Spirit of Hunger spoke. "Yes, my friend, I am Hunger."

"Have you come to kill me?" asked the dragonfly.

"No, I have not come to kill you. I am just wandering around aimlessly, hunting for a victim. You seem to be able to take care of yourself and get plenty to eat. I am looking for someone who is too lazy to work and is always thinking there is nothing to do. This person is a nuisance to the people about him and he should be gotten rid of. You are so happy and busy. You do not have time to get hungry."

Then they went their ways. The dragonfly went to hunt water, and the Spirit of Hunger went to hunt someone who was too lazy to work.

Dragonfly met bat (*jaa'abaní*) and told him of his meeting with the Spirit of Hunger. "Let's go and see if we can find him," said the bat. "I would like to see him."

They were flying along, hunting for the Spirit of Hunger and for water at the same time, when they saw an old woman sitting alone. She had spread out her robe and was sitting on it. They thought they would have a little fun, so they slipped up behind her and touched her. She did not look back to see who they were, but just ran away and left her robe. It turned into this plant with the blue flowers. The foolish old woman helped the people by leaving her robe. So every act counts for something and has a purpose in it.

When Wolfkiller asked about a plant with blue flowers, his grandfather told him a story about an old woman who jumped up when she was startled and left her robe lying on the ground.

The dragonfly and the bat went on their way and at last found the Spirit of Hunger near an anthill watching horned toad (*na'ashó'ïi dich'ízhii*) catching and eating ants. Just then, the Spirit of Hunger said to himself, "I see he is no good to me either. He is able to take care of himself."

Soon the dragonfly and the bat got tired of watching the horned toad and went on their way to hunt water. The Spirit of Hunger went on his way, still looking for a victim.

"This is the story of one little plant, my grandson. There are many more stories of plants, as there are of animals and birds and bugs and everything else about you."

Courage

The next day we were looking for something to ask Grandfather about when we saw a beautiful little yellow bird flying around in the sunflowers. The sunflowers were very pretty with their bright yellow petals and black centers, and the little yellow bird was having a good time flying around among them. We talked about the bird and decided to ask Grandfather to tell us about him that night.

That afternoon the black clouds began to come up over the red mesas in the west. They piled up higher and higher. Soon the sky began to get dark above us, and we could see streaks of lightning around us. It was still early in the afternoon, but we decided to take the sheep home, as they were getting very restless. They also knew that a big storm was coming and began to run here and there and bleat. We got them together and started them for home. By that time it was dark all around us, and the flashes of lightning came nearer and nearer to us with great claps of thunder.

We were very much afraid of the lightning, as we had seen our uncle struck down near our hogan while he was working in the cornfield just the previous year. Because of that, we had been compelled to leave that place where our hogan was. We did not like our new home place as well as the old one, but the people said we must not think about the past

To the west of Monument Valley are red mesas bisected by canyons. This is the mouth of Tsegi Canyon. A Navajo sweat house is nestled in the juniper trees in the foreground.

when it was unpleasant unless it could help someone see where their faults were. Remembering the death of our uncle did not help anyone, so we had to forget it.

Nevertheless, now that we saw the great flashes of lightning, we were afraid and began to think of the awful time we had gone through. I did not talk about it to my brother, and he said nothing, but I imagined the terrible storm of the other year. I could see my uncle start to run for the hogan, but when he reached the edge of the cornfield, a great zigzag of lightning came from the heavens and he fell. We had to live in the hogan where we were at the time for four nights and could not disturb the body. I could not sleep. I could see my uncle lying there on his face where he had fallen, and we could not eat until the day after he had been killed.

The lightning now came closer and closer, and the rain was coming in sheets. We were drenched. We hurried the sheep as much as we could, but they scattered in spite of us. We had a wash to cross before we reached the hogan, and we knew that we must get across it before the flood came. The storm had come from up the wash, and we knew a flood would soon be coming. We began to cry and were so much afraid.

At last we reached the wash and got the sheep across it just in time. As we climbed out on the other side, we heard the roar of water just above us. It came rolling down toward us like a great bank of mud, all covered with foam and with sticks and branches of trees floating on it. We were so glad to be safely across the wash that we forgot our fear of the lightning for a few minutes. We watched the flood sweep by and saw the soft bank of the wash crumble and fall into the water, making it muddier. Every storm was making the wash deeper and wider.

Our grandfather came to us from the hogan. He said he was glad we had crossed the wash before the flood came. The storm was letting up now, as it was sweeping on toward the north. We took the sheep to the corral and went into the hogan to get dry and warm.

We told Grandfather that we had been very much afraid of the lightning.

"Can't I teach you not to think of the things you do not want to happen?" he said. "Have I not told you that things like the lightning, the wind, and the rain are not our business? They strike where they will, and we have no control over them. When we see them coming, we must have the thought in our hearts that we will be safe from them, and it is good to say a prayer that they may be sent around us. It is always good to pray that we may be made stronger, but fear, as I have told you, is a part of the evil spirit, and it will poison you so that you will not be able to think of the things about you. Now that the storm has gone by us, I want you to come outside the hogan with me."

We went with him. He told us he wanted us to watch the storm as it passed over the rock to the north of us. "See how beautiful it really is," he said. "How black the clouds are. See the streaks of white lightning coming down. See the rocks over which it has passed—how they glisten. And you can see how fresh and green the cornfields, grass, and trees are now. We needed the storm to make things beautiful."

By the time the water stopped running in the washes, darkness had come. The storm had cleared and cooled the air. We went into the hogan where our mother was roasting green corn in the coals for our supper. After eating, we settled down for the night.

We talked a little about the storm and were at peace. Then we told our grandfather about the little bird we had seen. We asked him to tell us its story.

The Sunflower Patch

Mr. Oriole and Mr. Bluebird (*hastiin tsídiłtsoii* and *hastiin dólii*) had their nests on the edge of a large sunflower patch. The oriole lived on the west side where the sunflowers were nice and green and all in blossom, and the bluebird lived on the east side where the sunflowers were all brown and the blossoms had gone to seed.

Mr. Bluebird was a rather happy-go-lucky sort of a fellow, with a drab, slate-colored coat. He had a fine string of blue beads that he thought a great deal of and with which he amused himself. One day he took his beads with him as he flew from branch to branch. He kept tossing them up and catching them, having a great time all by himself.

From his nest on the west side of the sunflower patch, Mr. Oriole saw the bluebird amusing himself with his blue beads. "I just wonder what that crazy bird is doing over there, hopping from one branch of that sunflower to another, tossing something blue up and down," he said to himself. "I wonder what those blue things are. They must be his beads. If they are beads, they are very pretty—much prettier than the ones I have. I wish I had some nice blue beads."

Wind overheard him talking to himself and whispered to him, "You are horrid to envy the bluebird for his beads when you have such a pretty place for your nest. See how nice and green the sunflowers are on this side, and how yellow their blossoms are. Are they not beautiful with their black-and-yellow centers? Now look at the other side of the patch. See how dry and dead they are over there. Some folks cannot be satisfied with the blessings they have at home. They must envy someone else's few blue beads. If you had those beads, you would want some yellow ones."

The oriole would not listen, and he started around the north end of the sunflower patch to pay the bluebird a visit. Just as he reached the north end of the patch, a rattlesnake rattled and frightened him very badly. He jumped back, exclaiming, "Oh my!" When backing away he fell over a stone into some yellow mud. At one end of the mud puddle, under the water, was some coal. His head fell into this. His coat, which was previously gray, was now dyed yellow and the top of his head was black.

The oriole splashed around in the mud and made a great deal of noise, but he kept getting in deeper. The bluebird had heard him say, "Oh my!" and now he heard the noise he was making while splashing around in the mud. He started at once to his rescue. Going around the north end of the sunflower patch, he came to the place where the rattlesnake was. The rattlesnake rattled again, and the bluebird jumped back in fright. He dropped his coat into some blue mud that was nearby. He picked it up and tried to wring the mud and water from it, but could not get it out. Although he tried and tried, he could do nothing with it.

While he was working with it, Mr. Blue Snake (*hastiin tł'iish dootł'izh*) came along. "What are you doing, my friend?" he asked.

"Oh, nothing," the bluebird replied. "I'm only trying to get this nasty blue mud out of my coat. I came over to help that bird out of the mud, and, just as I got near this nasty blue mud hole, a horrid rattlesnake rattled and frightened me. I jumped backwards and dropped my coat in the mud. Now I can't get it cleaned off."

"Let it stay in, my cousin," the blue snake said. "I think it is very pretty that way. See—my coat is that color. Don't you think it is very pretty?"

"Yes, I think your coat is pretty," the bluebird replied, "but I don't think I would look as good in blue as you do."

"Just put your coat on and see if you don't like it," said the snake.

The bluebird said he would try it on to see how he liked it. He took his hat off, laid it on a stone by the side of the mud hole, and started to put on his coat when his hat fell into the mud. He took it out, and it was all blue just like his coat. He smoothed out the sleeves and then the rest of his coat. He looked at himself and rather liked his looks, so he put on his hat and smoothed it down over his head until it fit perfectly.

The blue snake said, "I think you look fine in blue." He called Mr. Hummingbird (*hastiin dahiitįhí*) and told him to come and look at the bluebird and see if he did not like his new coat of blue. The hummingbird came, and when he saw the bluebird, he laughed at first. Then he said he thought the bluebird did indeed look fine.

Mr. Bluebird then got some pitch and glued his hat and coat to his neck so there would never again be any danger of their coming off if a rattlesnake frightened him again. "If they fell off again, they might fall in some nasty gray or brown mud, and I certainly would hate to have a gray coat again," he said.

All this time the oriole was still stuck in the mud. He was laughing at the bluebird for dropping his coat and hat into the blue mud. The bluebird and the hummingbird went over to help him get out, but he kept on laughing. Finally, the hummingbird became angry and slapped him. "You horrid child, stop laughing until we can get you out of this nasty yellow mud," he said. The hummingbird slapped the oriole so hard that he made his legs very short, but still the oriole did not stop laughing. The hummingbird then slapped him in the mouth. "Stop the laughing," he demanded. This time he struck him on the bill, making it very short.

The oriole still kept on laughing. The bluebird and the hummingbird were trying their best to get him out, and the hummingbird slipped and fell into some nasty gray mud that was alongside the yellow mud. It made his coat all gray. All the other animals that were watching felt sorry for Mr. Hummingbird because he was a good man and was always trying to help someone out of trouble—all, that is, except the oriole. The oriole laughed and laughed at the hummingbird. "Your stomach looks very funny and round with all that gray mud on it," he said.

At last, the animals got the oriole out of the mud and stood him on dry ground. Mr. Frog (*haastin ch'ał*) came over from where he had been watching. "You deserve a beautiful coat for all you have done for this ungrateful oriole," he said to Mr. Hummingbird. "We will, of course, have to overlook his actions—he is such a child. When he grows up, he may act differently. We all hope so. He has a pretty yellow coat that he does not deserve. However, it must be for the best, as everything is, although we do not know it at the time. He got us into trouble just because he was not satisfied with what he had at home. He wanted the bluebird's beads and was coming over to try to get them when he heard the rattlesnake and fell into the mud. However, time will tell. There must be some good in him or he would not have come out so well, and we do not have the right to find fault with what happens in this world. You do deserve a pretty coat, Mr. Hummingbird, and I am going to give you the most beautiful thing I have for your coat. Here they are; let me put them on for you." So saying, the frog put pieces of the rainbow over the back of the hummingbird. Since they were not large enough to cover him all over, his stomach is still gray, but the rest of his coat shines in the sun like a rainbow.

After the story was finished, we all waited for Grandfather to speak again. He sat quietly for a while and then said, "I have been waiting for you to ask me some questions, my grandchildren. Do you now see what trouble we can cause by wanting the things someone else has? You are not the only ones who are hurt by your evil thoughts—they cause trouble for many others.

"The hummingbird and the bluebird got their reward for the help they gave the other people. Just because they went to help someone who was in trouble, they have beautiful coats now. So if you can ever help anyone, try to do it and you will receive your reward. It may look as if you had done more harm than good at first, but you will see the purpose sometime."

"Grandfather, I wish someone would get into trouble so that I could help them and get a reward like the bluebird and the hummingbird," I said.

"Hush, my grandson. You must not say things like that. That is an evil thought and it will cause you trouble. Opportunities do not come to you when you wish someone else harm so that you will gain something by their unhappiness. People who wish for such things are always the ones who need help when the time comes. If they send out too many evil thoughts, they are beyond help. People who are always trying to get something for nothing and wishing for something they do not deserve will find themselves without anything and with no friends in the end. My grandson, try to remember this: try to give to people all you can and you will receive your reward. It is late now, but tomorrow night I will tell you another story."

I found I was very tired when I lay down to sleep. I thought of what Grandfather had told me about fear poisoning a person, how foolish I had been to be afraid of the lightning, and how it must have been fear and my other evil thought that was making me so tired now. I resolved to try never to think of fear or evil again.

Generosity

The next evening Grandfather continued our training by telling us another story.

The Ant and the Wasp

Many years ago there lived at a place called Water Path a colony of red ants. Nearby, at a place called Strength of the Rocks, lived a wasp. On this particular day, the red ant was gathering seeds from the plants for his winter food. The wasp took his bow and arrow and went to hunt for meat for his winter food, as he did not care for the seeds if he could secure meat. He was lucky and killed two rabbits, a rat, a gopher, and a prairie dog. As he was returning home, he happened to pass close to the home of the red ant. As he drew near, the ant saw him. "You must not come any nearer my house," he shouted. "This is my food, which I have gathered."

Now, when the red ant spoke in this manner, it made the wasp angry. "I will come as near as I please," the wasp replied. "I am not afraid of you, and I will eat the food if I care to. It is gathered from the plants around here, and the plants are as much mine as they are yours."

"The plants may be as much yours as mine, but you did not do the work of gathering and piling them up," the red ant exclaimed. "They are mine. You can go and gather your own seeds or hunt your own rabbits, prairie dogs, gophers, or rats, but you cannot have my seeds that I have already gathered." At this, the wasp picked up a handful of dirt and threw it at the red ant.

The black ant saw them quarreling. "You must stop quarreling," he said. "There is plenty of food of all kinds around here without arguing about it, and you have plenty of time to gather food. If you were gathering it now instead of quarreling, you could already have gathered enough food to last both of you a full day."

To this the wasp replied, "I don't care. It was he who started the quarrel, and I am going to eat this food for him." Picking up another handful of dirt, he threw it at the red ant.

At this, the red ant became very angry, and, running at the wasp, caught him around the waist. The wasp threw his arms around the ant, and they squeezed and squeezed each other so tight that both of them nearly broke in two. That is why the ant and the wasp have such small waists today.

Then the hummingbird came along. As he came up, the wasp fell and bumped his head on a rock, raising a lump that is there to this day. The hummingbird said to them, "Don't fight anymore. That is no way for old men to act."

As a matter of fact, both the wasp and the red ant were boys, but the hummingbird called them old men to flatter them. They paid no attention and kept on fighting. The hummingbird caught hold of the red ant's arm and pulled him off the wasp. The red ant was glad to quit. As the hummingbird did this, he got some of the yellow pollen from his legs above the red ant's eyes. That is what makes the yellow streak above the ant's eyes to this day.

The wasp got up and caught the hummingbird around the neck with one arm and around the legs with the other. He doubled him up into a ball until the hummingbird cried out, "Ouch! That hurts!" But the wasp paid no attention to him and just continued holding him until his own arms and legs had stretched so much that he could no longer hold the hummingbird. That is the reason that the wasp's legs are so long.

When he could no longer hold the hummingbird with his arms and legs, he sat down on him. While he was sitting there, along came the nighthawk. "Say, Mr. Wasp," he said, "don't kill that man. Let him go." The nighthawk did not know what to do, so he went over to a sunflower nearby and pulled off two petals. He slipped up and pasted them to the shoulders of the wasp. "See what I have put on your back. You can fly now." Before this, the wasp had no wings.

The wasp looked around over his shoulder at the two sunflower petals and asked, "Who said that to me?" The nighthawk told him that it was a message from the God of the North.

"But what am I to do with these yellow petals on my back?"

"You are to fly with them," replied the nighthawk.

The wasp looked into the heavens, saying, "I think it might be nice to fly. I will try it." He stretched his new wings and flew to the sky.

As he rose up, the red ant looked at him and said, "How nice it must be to be able to fly. I do not think it is fair to give those pretty wings to the wasp. It was he who fought the longest."

To this, the hummingbird replied, "Although the wasp did fight longer and harder than you and squeezed you so hard that he made you very small, he got his punishment. You nearly cut him in two and he stretched his arms and legs so long that they look as if they are nearly ready to break. He has a big lump on his head where he hit the rock. Now you were the one who started the quarrel by your evil thoughts and your stinginess. You were the one who told him not to come near your house, and that the food was yours. Even if it is a little work to gather food, it is not polite not to ask one to eat when he comes to your house. Besides that, the wasp had plenty of food of his own, and I do not think he even thought of taking yours, as he would much rather have meat than your seeds. He does not eat seeds if he can get meat. You had to be suspicious just because you had done a little work gathering your food. In this world, we must help each other or we cannot get along. After this, when anyone comes to your house, you should be kind and polite."

The wasp had returned and stood listening to the hummingbird. When he finished talking, he went to him and said, "You are a good man to forgive me for hurting you and saying it was not my fault. I should have minded my own business, going my way and not listening to the red ant when he spoke to me as he did. I was not angry when I threw the dirt at him. I was just teasing him. I see that it will not do to tease people and do things that we do not mean. I thank you, my brother, for forgiving me, and I hope my experience will teach me a lesson that I will remember. I hope I will not be so foolish as to fight again about nothing."

Then they all shook hands and started for their different homes.

As Mr. Nighthawk was going along the trail, he came to the house of Mrs. Dove, who was washing her clothes. "I am very thirsty, my friend," he said. "I see you have some water there. Will you not give me a drink?" Mrs. Dove handed him her water jug, and he drank and drank. When he had finished, he handed the jug back to her. There was still plenty of water in it.

"How silly the ant was to be so stingy with his food," the nighthawk said. "He must not have known that we will always be provided for if we will try to remember to be pleasant to everyone."

Mrs. Dove asked him what he was talking about, and he told her about the trouble he had just gone through. "That is why I am so thirsty and hungry. I have not been home to get any food or water yet." At this, Mrs. Dove brought out a dish of grass seeds and gave it to him to eat. He ate and ate, but the dish was still full. When he finished, he gave it back to her and she had all she wanted.

"I must be on my way," said the nighthawk. "Is there anything I can do for you? Mrs. Dove told him there was nothing, so he started on.

He soon came to a pool of water, and the mud hen came out and confronted him. "Where are you going?" he asked.

"I am going home," he replied.

"You are telling me an untruth," said the mud hen. "Now tell me what you are doing around here."

The nighthawk said that he was telling the truth, but the mud hen would not believe it. He caught the nighthawk by the corners of his mouth and tore it very badly. That is the reason that he now has such a large mouth.

At this, the nighthawk caught the mud hen by his bill and squeezed it down flat. While they were scuffling, the nighthawk dropped a bag of gum that was tied to his belt, and the mud hen stepped on it and made the webs between his toes.

They finally quit, and the nighthawk got some blue mud and put it on the mud hen's bill to heal it, making it all blue. The mud hen then went and gathered some yellow ochre with which to heal the nighthawk's mouth, making it all yellow as it is to this day.

"The story I have told you, my grandson, is to teach you not to be selfish and stingy. Those who give what they have will always have plenty for themselves. And another thing—you must not think people are doing or thinking something bad about you just because they are going about their business and not paying attention to you. When you accuse people of doing wrong, you put thoughts into their minds that they did not have before. You harm yourself and all the people about you. Just think how many people got into the quarrel who were going about their own business.

"Another thing the story tells you is when the fight was over, the two who were fighting did not know what they were fighting about. That is the way it is with most fights. When it is over, we wonder why we fought."

As the days went by, I thought a great deal about the story and Grandfather's advice about not thinking foolish thoughts or getting angry about little things.

The elders gave the young people thoughtful advice, such as to not be overly suspicious or angry about trivial things.

Body Heat

It was almost time to harvest the corn, and all the people were busy getting ready for the harvest. As we herded the sheep, we could see the bright red and yellow splashes of color on the mountainside where the oaks and aspens were turning. They looked beautiful among the dark green of the spruce and pine. Soon they would lose their leaves and look gray.

Before this year, I had hated the winters, but now I knew that they came to make the summers more beautiful. One day I thought about this while we were herding the sheep, and when we returned to the hogan that night, I asked Grandfather if it was true.

"You are right, my grandson," he said. "The winters do make the summers more beautiful. Our Mother Earth sleeps through the winters and rests for the work she will have to do the next summer. That is why we count the winters and not the summers, as we count the nights and not the days. The earth is sleeping all winter, so she does not know what is going on. A year of her life has not gone by until she awakens in the spring, as a day of our lives has not gone by until we awake in the morning after a night's sleep. So the days come and go and the years come and go."

The harvest time came, and our people had much work to do, as this year they had to dig new pits for storing the corn. They dug them some distance from the hogan.

I asked my mother why they dug them far away. "My son," she answered, "they are not dug near the hogan as they would be too easy to find if someone made a raid on us. Have you never noticed that we always dig them near some rocks? This is so we can go to them and not leave any tracks for people to follow. We learned this many years ago. Though there have not been any raids on us for some years now, we never know when a raiding party will come again. If they should come, they would take the food we have in the hogan, but they would not get all of it."

The corn was soon harvested and put into the pits, which were lined with corn shucks. There was much corn this year, so we had several large pits. The pits were put some distance apart. Mother explained that this was for the same reason that the pits were not near the hogan. If a raiding party should come and find one of the pits, they would think that was all of the food we had and they would go away and leave the rest of it.

By the time the corn was all stored, the frost had come to open the burrs of the pinyon nuts. We moved into the mountains to gather them up. That year the nuts were plentiful, and we gathered as many as we could. We worked for a whole moon. Then it got very cold on the mountain, so we moved down to our hogan and settled for the winter.

Wolfkiller learned to face the cold of winter and to appreciate the cycles of the seasons.

One morning, a few days after we had returned to our hogan, Mother woke us at dawn. She said that it was snowing and we must go out and roll in the snow. We complained that we did not like to roll in the cold snow.

"My children, that is the reason I want you to do it. It is because it seems cold to you. The snow will be with us for several moons now, and if you roll in it and treat it as a friend, it will not seem nearly as cold to you. You have rolled in the snow every winter since you were babies. Why should you not want to do it now?"

"Mother, I am sorry I said what I did. I did not know why we always rolled in the snow until now. I am glad you have told me."

We went out and did what Mother told us to do. It did not seem half as cold to me as it had before.

After breakfast, Mother cut shoes out of a sheepskin and sewed them on our feet with the wool sides in. Although they did not look very pretty, they were warm and would keep our feet dry while we herded the sheep. She belted our robes around our waists and put our headbands on nice and smooth so they would keep our foreheads warm. Our long hair would keep our ears and heads warm, and our robes would cover our hands. We saddled our burros that morning. We had been herding the sheep on foot all summer, but now that the winter had come, we had to use the burros again.

It snowed all day, but we did not mind. We shook the snow from our robes from time to time, as we had been taught to do, so the heat of our bodies would not melt it and get us wet.

That evening we returned to our warm hogan. The snowstorm continued all night. When dawn came, the snow was deep, but everyone was happy. Now the sheep would have to browse on the greasewood along the banks of the wash again.

PART II—EXPERIENCE

A Warning of Trouble

The winter passed quickly, and it was soon time to plant the corn again. The men started getting the fields ready.

Late one afternoon, as my brother and I sat watching the sheep, we looked up and noticed a thin line of smoke rising toward the heavens. It came from the top of a high rock far away. The air was very clear, and we could see it plainly. After a very short time, it disappeared. As we were discussing what it might mean, we saw it come and go again. Then we saw it a third time, and then a fourth. We watched for a long time, but did not see it again. We talked a great deal about it. "We will ask Grandfather about it tonight," I said.

That night, when everyone was sitting around the fire, we told the older people what we had seen. They were startled, and then I saw sadness come into their faces. For a while, no one spoke. They were very quiet, and I began to be frightened.

Then Grandfather spoke. "My grandson, it was a signal fire—the warning of trouble. I fear the evil spirit of war is coming. There has been some unrest ever since the raiding party I told you about some time ago went out and brought back the sheep and girls, but we had hoped the war would not come. We must still try not to add to our thoughts the thoughts of the ones who are causing us trouble. We must pray and work as before. Pray that the evil will miss us. We have done nothing to cause it, so we must let the ones who want war go their own way. We will stay at our own hogan and plant our corn and not worry about what is going on about us."

Some of the old people said, "If we go about our own business, it will not bother us. But even among us there may be some who secretly hope that they will see war. We hope not, and we must pray that their thoughts will change if they do have these evil thoughts."

Wolfkiller's family learned about the impending war from smoke signals sent by distant Navajo informants. They assigned a sentinel to keep watch for the signals.

At this, our visitors silently left the hogan and went to their own homes. When they were gone, Grandfather said, "My grandson, tomorrow I want you to watch the point on which you saw the smoke today. I want to know what the next signal will be."

"We will watch it and tell you what we see," I promised. "But will you tell us how they can make the smoke go up in such a thin column, and then stop, and then come again? And why was the smoke so white?"

"It is done, my grandson, by building a small fire and putting damp bark on it. Have you never noticed how white the smoke is from a damp fire and how it goes straight up? Then, when the smoke goes way up, they hold their robes over it for a while. Then they put more bark on and take the robe away. This they do four times. If it is dark when they want to send the signals, they do it with a blaze."

Before breakfast the next morning, Grandfather and some of the other old men met in our hogan and talked about the smoke. It was not as clear that day, and the people were worried that they would not be able to see the signal. They decided that someone must do nothing but watch for it all day, so they appointed one of the older boys to go a high point to do this. They asked my brother and me to watch as well.

All through the forenoon we saw nothing, but as the sun was dipping toward the west, the sky cleared in the east and we saw the signal.

This time it was two slender columns of smoke side by side. They came and went four times as they had the day before.

When we reached the hogan that evening, the people knew about the signals, as the sentinel also had seen them. They were all talking about what to do when we came in.

We asked Grandfather what the two signals meant. He said that it meant that they were calling a council. That night the people decided to send some of the old men to attend the council the next day.

The next morning we were all up early. The women fixed lunches of dried meat and corn bread for the men to take with them. They must not let themselves talk or think too much about trouble. We must still keep our thoughts running in the path of light.

For two days, we all went about our business and tried not to think about the fact that what we feared was coming to us soon. After we returned to the hogan on the second night, the old men came in. They were very quiet. All of the rest of the people were quiet, too. We all waited for what they would tell us about the council. We were very anxious for supper to be over so we could sit down and hear what they had to say. As soon as everything was finished, the people began coming into our hogan.

When we were seated around the fire, Grandfather spoke.

> My children, it is as we feared. The spirit of war is trying to walk into our land, but we must try to stop it. We do not want war, as I said before. We have done nothing to cause this thing, but some of the people have made another raid, and our chief, at what they call Washington, has sent us word that we must leave our land and go with the soldiers to a place far to the east. They say they will take care of us. Now I think the people who have brought this on themselves should be taken, but we who do not want to have trouble should not be taken away from a land we know and are contented to live in.
>
> We will go on with our planting and try to raise as much corn as we can. Then we can go back into the canyons to the west of us and live there as we have lived for many years. We will still fight for peace and try to stay in the path of light. Some of the people who called us to the council feel as we do about this thing. They do not want war, so we have decided to plant our corn, and then leave our fields and scatter our camps in the rock-walled canyons.

We will have to appoint some men as scouts and keep sentinels out to watch for signals—not for the same purpose as we sent out our scouts and kept our sentinels on the hills in years gone by, but for our protection. In times gone by, when we were at war, we kept the sentinels and scouts out to let us know when it was the best time for us to make an attack—to tell us where our enemy was and when they were off their guard. Now we will send our scouts and sentinels out to keep us posted so that we can move when the soldiers come near to us. We will hide so they cannot find us. We will continue to pray for peace as we have been praying ever since the rumor of war first started.

Now, my children, I have told you what the council was. A number of men who were at the council feel as we do, but some of the other ones want war. Our war chief thinks we should fight. He thinks that we are strong enough to fight as many soldiers as the enemy could send against us if we fight here in our own land. But we old men know that we are not as strong as they are—not because we have not the strength in our bodies, but because we haven't the guns and ammunition of the white men. Many of us have only our bows and spears with which to fight.

The war chief has told the people that, though the white men have many guns and cannons with which to fight us and have many soldiers, our people know the country. By sneaking up on these people, we can steal their food and horses and leave them in want so they will be too weak to fight. Another advantage we have of them, he says, is that we know where the water is and they do not. So he says we must cause as much trouble now as we can so they will come against us in the summertime, as in summer there is not much water—only in the springs and tanks in the rocks.

Now, my children, we who do not want war must hurry and get our corn planted. The Seed Basket is now in the heavens, so it is time to plant. We must work until late at night. We must get as much corn planted as possible. We do not know how long the war will last, and we must have food laid by for a siege.

For many days, the people worked until it was too dark for them to see any longer. They planted large fields that year.

Fighting the Evil Thought

One evening the people were talking about the news of the day. One of the men spoke.

> At the place we call Bear Water, a council has been held. The men who told us about it say that a man who is the chief of the soldiers from Bear Water has been talking to our people. He told them that if we will come in and go peaceably to the place they want us to go to, we will not have to fight, but if we will not go peaceably, they will send many soldiers and many big guns against us. Some of the people say they think it would be good to go, but some of them think as we do.
>
> As we have not done anything to cause the evil spirit to walk in our land, we cannot see why we should be punished. Of course, our past record is against us, as in years gone by it was the sanction of the whole tribe that our people went out and made the raids on the people of the villages. But the raids that have been made in the past few years have not been with the consent of most of us. Most of us have wanted peace, as we do now, but it remains to be seen whether we can have it.
>
> If in the end we have to go, we must do it with peace still in our hearts. We have planned to harvest as much corn as we can and keep away from the ones who want war. Our war chief is all for war, and he has many of the young men with him. These young men have never seen the sorrows of war, so they do not know what it is.

Then Grandfather spoke.

> My brothers, you feel as we do. I am glad there are others among us who are still fighting the evil thought. We are planning to move into the canyons west of us as soon as we finish planting our fields, which will be soon now. We hope the enemy will not find us. We hope our young men will not get the evil thought in their hearts

and go to join the war chief. If they do, it will mean that we will have to help them if they need us.

But we must not think of such things. We must still hope and pray that this evil will miss us. We must not talk too much about our fears, for if we do, we will put the evil thought into the minds of some of our people who do not think much about it now. We must all work together and try to stay in the path of light.

We will let our war chief and his band of men go to the place they want to go without us, as it is now too late to do anything for them. I do not feel anger in my heart against our chief who is at the place they call Washington.[3] Some of our people have brought the trouble on themselves and all the rest of us, as we who do not want to fight will have our troubles keeping out of the way of the ones who are for war, and out of the way of the soldiers. But we will try to keep out of their way as long as we can.

The stars are dipping toward the west. It would be good for all of us to rest now, as we will have our work to do tomorrow.

We all went to bed, but I could not sleep for a long time. I was thinking about all of the things the old men had said. I again thought of what Grandfather had said about the raids in the past being needed to save the life of the tribe, and now this other old man had said the same thing. I wanted to know what they meant by this and hoped that I could get my grandfather or mother to tell me the story sometime.

The Hogan Song

One evening, late that spring, we were all resting around the hogan door just after dark when I heard a faint sound from far away. As it came closer, I realized that it was someone singing. No one spoke, so I got up and started to climb up onto a high knoll to see who it was.

My mother called me back. "My son," she said, "have you no manners? You must come and sit down. Can you not hear them singing the hogan song? They are friends, or they would not give us any warning.

3 The U.S. president.

You must sit quietly and wait for them. If they saw you watching them, they would not be pleased. It would be as if you were spying on them, and we do not spy on our friends."

I came back and sat down. "I am sorry, Mother. I will not do it again," I said.

Soon two men I had never seen before rode up. They shook hands with all of us. Then Mother put a robe down for them to sit on. She built up the fire, which was out in front of the hogan now that the days were warm, and began cooking some meat for the men. They told my father and grandfather that they had come some distance that day. I was anxious to know what they wanted, but knew that we would have to wait until they were ready to tell us. As soon as their supper was ready, my mother set it before them.

Visitors arrived at Wolfkiller's hogan dressed in their finest outfits to ask for his sister's hand in marriage. The handmade silver, turquoise, white shell, and coral jewelry that these men are wearing were highly prized.

After they finished eating, they smoked for a few minutes. Then one of them turned to my mother and said, "I have come to ask for your daughter. I have a nephew who is old enough to be married. We have heard that your daughter is the kind of a girl we would like him to marry, and now that I see her, I am pleased with her. She is good looking and modest, as I can see. You have not seen my nephew, but I think if you saw him you would be willing to let your daughter marry him. I have brought my friend here along to tell you about him."

Grandfather then said that he knew both of these men and we could take their word for anything they told us. He asked the men if the young man who had helped in the ceremony he had performed at their hogan was the one they were talking about. They said that he was. Grandfather told Mother that he thought he was a good man and that she could trust him.

Mother agreed that she could trust him.

"We will give you one string of white and turquoise beads and one string of red beads of five strands each, and two horses for your daughter," the first man said.

"That is good," said Mother. "You are generous."

"When do you think we should bring my nephew here to your hogan?" the man asked. "The bluebirds are nesting now. We both have many friends, and there are nests nearby, so we could perform that part of the ceremony soon."

"I think we could have it in about fifteen days," Mother said.

The next morning the two men started for their hogans. Grandfather wanted them to stay and visit for a few days, but they said they had much work to do and must be on their way.

That evening I asked my mother what the man meant when he said, "The bluebirds are nesting." She explained that when a couple of our young people were to be married, the family and friends of both the boy and the girl are asked to hunt a bluebird's nest and watch the nest until one of the birds comes to feed the young. Then they snare it, sprinkle pollen on it, and let it go. Then they watch for the mate and sprinkle pollen on it, too. This is done to make the marriage more binding. If a girl is of marriageable age at any other time of the year, the people either wait until the summer comes to let the couple get married, or they perform the ceremony as soon after the marriage as they can.

The fifteen days before our sister's wedding went by very quickly. After the men finished planting the corn, they built her a hogan. Grandfather explained that, even though we would be leaving this place very soon, she would need a hogan when we came back here to live after the trouble was over.

Everyone was busy for two days getting ready for the wedding. My mother and sister finished the blankets they were weaving for the new hogan. Then they had to grind much corn, as there would be many people to feed. My sister ground the mush corn for her wedding.

On the evening of the wedding, we came in early with the sheep. Mother told us we might do this so we could be at the hogan when the wedding party arrived, which would be just before sunset. Many people had already gathered at the hogan by the time we reached it. The women were sitting around watching my mother, who was helping to make the mush for the ceremony, and all of the men were sitting around in my sister's new hogan, where the wedding was to take place.

Soon after we came in, we saw the bridegroom and his family coming. They rode up to where my sister was making the mush, and then they came over to greet us. First they shook hands with my mother, and then with all the rest of us. The bridegroom was introduced to my mother, and then to my sister. Then they gave Mother the horses and the beads they had brought for her. After this, all of the men went to the new hogan to wait with the rest of the men for the ceremony.

Soon the mush was ready, and Mother put it into a basket. She then called to Grandfather to come and conduct my sister and the rest of the women to the wedding. My sister was given the basket of mush to carry, and Grandfather led the party to the hogan. My sister went next to Grandfather, and the rest of the women followed her—all except for Mother, who could not see her son-in-law. She stayed at her own hogan.

When all the people had sat down in the new hogan, my sister and the young man she was to marry sat down side by side with the basket of mush in the center of the hogan in front of them. They faced the east.

Grandfather sat down on the opposite side of the basket, facing the west. He made a cross of pollen on the mush. The pollen was from all the plants, and it represented happiness, prosperity, and fertility. When the cross was drawn, Grandfather told the young man to take a pinch of mush with the fingers of his right hand and eat it. Then my sister took a pinch. They did this four times, eating from a different section of the

The young man who was to marry Wolfkiller's sister came to meet her family. He was probably about the age of this boy, who is characteristically shy and wears his long hair in a knot.

basket each time. Then the mush was passed to the rest of us to finish, as all of it must be eaten.

After this, Grandfather told my sister and her husband that they must try to do everything they could for each other and work to lead the right kind of life and stay in the path of light. Some of the other people also talked to them and told them how they should live.

Then the ceremony was over, and we all went out and left them alone. We went to Mother's hogan where much food was awaiting us. One of the women took some food to the new hogan for the bride and groom. The people feasted and talked far into the night. The next morning they all went to their separate hogans and our lives went on as before. We all missed our sister's presence in our hogan, but we knew she was near and we could go to see her every day.

Hiding Out

After our corn crop was established, we moved to a place where we would be among the rocks. Soon after we moved there, we saw some signal fires one night, calling a council. The next day Father and Grandfather went to the council. When they came back after three days, they told us it was as they had feared. The soldiers were going about in our land and had had some fights with some of our people. A number of the war chiefs had been killed or wounded, but the rest had gotten away into the mountains.

"Now we must keep our sentinels out and send out our scouts," Grandfather said. "We will try to stay away from this trouble."

For many days, we hid in the canyons where we could find feed for our sheep and horses. The men went to the cornfields from time to time. The rain came and made the corn grow very fast. The women wove blankets and gathered grass and weed seeds to store for the winter, as this year the men would not be able to go out to hunt as they had each year before. They would not want to leave the women and children alone long enough to hunt.

From time to time, the scouts came in with the news of more and more trouble.

A labyrinth of canyons provided a hiding place for Wolfkiller's family when the soldiers came near.

The summer went by, and it was again time for the harvest. Everyone worked very hard to get the harvest over as soon as possible. The corn was taken to the box canyons some distance to the west of us. We had also grown some pumpkins, and the women dried and stored them in buckskin bags. We were all as happy as we could be at a time like this, as we had food enough to last us a long time.

Soon the winter came again. We lived in the canyons and moved from one place to another. I now saw what war could be. We could not have our nice, warm hogan because we were moving so much. Then the heavy snow came and we were not so much afraid. Grandfather said we could build a hogan now, but we must build it among the rocks so that it could not easily be discovered. The rocks would serve as a chimney to carry the smoke up to the top of the mesas so anyone in the canyon would not be able to smell it.

From time to time, the scouts went out. Each time they came back, they told us that there was no news. The winter went by, and when spring came, the people planted again. We had much food left, but we knew we must keep up the supply.

Joy

One night our mother and some of the other women were called to our sister's hogan, and our brother-in-law came to our hogan. They told us that our sister was sick and our mother and father must be with her.

The next morning she had a baby boy. We were anxious to see him, and we went to her hogan as soon as we were up.

Mother and Grandfather were getting some fir boughs ready to make a cradle board for the baby. Grandfather took a knife of white shell from his medicine bag and began to chant. His words were:

For you I make a smooth cradle.

He said this over and over as he smoothed the sticks, first with the knife of white shell, then with a quartz crystal. When he had finished smoothing the sticks, Mother got some strings of buckskin from a bag and helped him tie the sticks together for the back of the board. Then they tied loops along the sides. Across the head of the board they tied a stick that Grandfather had smoothed and bent for a bow. Then they tied some short sticks together and attached them to the foot of the board for a footrest.

Grandfather began to chant again. This time his words were:

For you I have made a smooth cradle.

He chanted this four times.

When this chant was completed, he held the cradle board with the head toward the east, and he started to pray:

Son of the Goddess of Sunset,
Spirit of the Pollen Boy,
God of Life,
Peaceably let him go.

He then sprinkled pollen four times on the side of the cradle board from the foot to the head, each time saying the prayer.

Next, he sprinkled pollen up the center of the cradle board four times and said this prayer each time:

Spirit of the Pollen Boy,
Voice of the Pollen Boy,
Head of the Pollen Boy.

Then he sprinkled the back with pollen and said this prayer:

Spirit of the God of Dawn,
Voice of the God of Dawn,
Head of the God of Dawn.

He finished by sprinkling the foot of the cradle while saying this prayer:

Spirit of the God of Sunset,
Voice of the God of Sunset,
Head of the God of Sunset.

Then Mother took the cradle and put some shredded bark on it, which she covered with a blanket. On the front of the bow, she tied buckskin to cover the baby's face. Then she put the baby in the cradle, covered him with a blanket, and laced him in with a buckskin thong, running it back and forth through the loops along the sides.

Now that he was in the cradle, Grandfather said another prayer:

I have made a cradle for you, my son;
May you live to a great old age;
Of the rays of the earth I have made the back;
The side loops I have made of the sunbeams;
The bow I have made of the rainbow;
The footboard I have made of the sundogs;
The blanket I have made of the black clouds;
The bed I have made of the black fog;
The lace I have made of the lightning;
The cover I have made of the dawn.

Grandfather then said another prayer:

God of the Dawn, with your strength let him stand;
God of the Dawn, let him stand with you;
God of the Dawn, with the strength of the corn, let him stand with you;
Let him stand with the white corn strength;
With the strength of the corn-bird, strength of the corn and the dawn;
Harvest Fly Boy, Pollen Boy, let him have shoes like the Harvest Fly;
Let him have leggings like the Harvest Fly;

Let him have a robe like the Harvest Fly;
Let him have a cap like the Harvest Fly;
Let him have feathers like the Harvest Fly;
Let his voice be beautiful like the Harvest Fly;
God of Pollen of Life, stand before him;
Walk before him;
Goddess of Harvest, Harvest Fly Maiden, stand behind him;
God of Speech, go back and forth before him;
Go with him to his home;
On a blanket of pollen let the cradle rest;
Let him drink of the springs of the earth;
Pollen, pollen of all the plants of the earth, let him eat;
Of the pollen of the water and the pollen of the mountains, let him eat.

When the prayer was ended, the ceremony was over and we went to our own hogan. We asked our mother to tell us about the ceremony. She said it was a very long story and she could not tell us about it then, but she would tell us about the making of the first cradle sometime. This was something new to learn about. I thought a great deal about it from time to time, but everyone was too busy to talk to me much.

Wolfkiller's sister had a baby, who brought great joy to the family. This young mother is weaving an exceptionally fine blanket while her child, secured in a cradle board, watches contentedly.

Surrender

When the summer rains came again and the corn was growing well, the scouts began to bring in news of the many soldiers who were coming against us and the efforts of our people to fight them. We still hoped that we would be spared this trouble.

One day a scout ran into camp and fell down exhausted. We waited as he caught his breath and was able to speak.

"We are lost," he said. "The enemy has brought Utes to help them track us down, and they are coming nearer. They are cutting down the cornfields and killing the old people who cannot travel. They have taken many of the people out."

After hearing this, Grandfather and the rest of the old people sat with their heads bowed for a long time. They were very quiet and sad.

Then Grandfather spoke. "We will try for a while longer to keep out of this trouble, but if the time comes when we think there is no other way out, we will surrender and go quietly with those people. They will be decent to us if we do not fight. After all, we have brought this on ourselves."

For a few days, we did not get much rest. As we moved farther and farther back into the canyon, the soldiers and Utes came nearer and nearer. The sentinels came in and told us that they had seen the dust of many people moving and could see their campfires. As we moved, the men sent the women, children, and sheep over the rocky ridges. Then they came along behind them, walking backward and brushing out their tracks with boughs of trees at places where we crossed sand. They hoped that by doing this we could avoid being discovered.

Each night the men climbed to the top of the mesa to watch for signals. One evening I went with them. The stars were dipping far toward the west before we saw any signals. When they came, there were four fires in a row, and they came four times. Then we all started for the hogan. Everyone went quietly—no one spoke. When we reached the camp, it was nearly dawn. Grandfather awakened the women and children and told them that it was no use to hide any longer, as the four fires meant that we were surrounded.

The men sat down and talked while the women cooked breakfast. They decided that three of the old men would go up that night to the camp of the soldiers and tell them we were ready to go with them. They said that the camp was not far from us.

"We will start as soon as the night comes," said Grandfather.

"Why do you go at night?" I asked.

He explained that they were afraid of the Utes who were with the soldiers. The Utes would welcome the chance to kill as many of our people as they could if our people came while it was light.

The sheep were kept in the rocks all day, and some of the men slept while the others kept watch. It seemed a long time before the night came. Everyone was very quiet, and no fires were built. We ate bread and dried meat that had been stored for a time like this.

As soon as the night came, the three old men stole silently out of the camp and were gone. We did not sleep much that night, as we were all nervously waiting for them to return. They did not come until the afternoon of the next day, and we had been very much worried for fear that the Utes had killed them.

When they came in, some soldiers were with them. This was the first time that I had ever seen a white man. They looked very strange to me, but I did not fear them as I had thought I would. They did not seem so bad. They had no Utes with them.

We were told to get ready to go with these people. We were to take everything we wanted to take. We were all busy for the rest of the day. The men got the horses and put them in the rocks for the night.

The next morning the horses were saddled and packed with the robes and food that we wanted to take with us. We could not take the corn we had in the pits, but the white men told us we would not need it, as they would give us plenty of food.

One white man who was with these people could speak our language pretty well. We could not understand anything the others said. The man who could speak to us told us that we would have no trouble from now on. We went with them with no fear in our hearts, but we all felt sad that we would be leaving the land we all knew and loved for a land that would be strange to us.

For the first few days, everything seemed strange. The soldiers sounded like a flock of birds in a tree when they talked, and their clothes were so odd. They did not wear robes like our people. I was interested in

After avoiding capture for more than a year, Wolfkiller's family and neighbors finally realized that they had to surrender to the soldiers. They gathered to discuss their fate.

their blue coats and pants and the strange things they wore on their heads. They did not wear headbands. I thought, as we rode to their camp, that this would be a strange life, but I was not going to complain. We were not suffering, and I knew that it must be for the best, or it would not have come to us.

When we reached their camp, I saw a wagon and a big gun. I asked Grandfather about these things and he told me what they were. I said I would like to see the soldiers shoot the big gun. He replied that he did not want to hear me say anything like that again and hoped I would never see them shoot it.

We stayed in the soldiers' camp that night. Grandfather told us how the three old men had slipped into the camp two nights before.

> When we came near the camp, we saw some Utes and one white man with the horses and mules. We crawled up as close as we dared to, but we were afraid to get very near them. We looked at the stars. I was wishing the people who were herding would soon get tired.

We could hear the Utes talking to each other once in a while, but most of the time they sat quietly on their horses and watched.

I started up over some rocks, and a small stone broke loose and rattled down to the bottom. I saw the Utes raise their heads and listen. I lay very quiet, but one of the Utes started toward me, so I crawled farther away and hid behind the rocks. The other men who were with me had slipped around on the other side of the horses to see where we could get into the camp most easily, so I was alone. I was afraid the Ute would find me. He came very near me, but I was in the shadow of the rock so he did not see me.

He hunted around for such a long time that I was afraid the other men would come to where I was. It was very dark among the rocks, and I thought, if they come to hunt me and did not know the Ute was there, they would surely be killed. So I began to pray that they would not come. After a time, the Ute started back toward the horses and I could breathe again. Soon after this, the other men came to me. They said they had been near some of the horses, and they did not pay any attention to them. By this time, the stars were dipping toward the west. We crawled away some distance so we could talk to each other.

We decided that if the Utes did not sleep, we would go back to our camp. We waited until the stars were dipping far to the west, and then we crawled back near the horses again and we saw that the Utes were resting. We waited just a little longer and then slipped in among the horses. Some of the horses looked at us. We were afraid they would make a noise, but after a time they did not pay any attention to us. They kept on grazing as if we were not there.

When we got close to the camp, we saw a guard standing near us with a gun. We were frightened and lay quiet for a long time until he walked a little farther away. Then we went on. We were almost up to the tents when I passed one of the Utes who was sound asleep. I did not see him until I was very close to him as I passed by. I was so near him that I touched his braid as I passed. He did not stir, so I knew he did not hear me.

It was getting darker now, and I knew it would not be long before the dawn would come. We were almost to the tents, and I was glad and hoped the soldiers would soon be awake. We crawled up to one of the tents and lay down. We were very tired and were glad to be safely in the camp.

I was relieved when I saw the first white streak of dawn. A little while after that the bugle sounded and the soldiers began to stir in the tents. Soon a soldier came out of a tent near us. We went up to him and tried to tell him what we wanted, but he could not understand us. By this time, many of the soldiers were out, and they called the man who went with us to our hogans yesterday (the man who could speak our language). He asked us what we wanted, and we told him that we were tired of hiding and wanted to go with the soldiers to the place they wanted to take us to.

Soon the chief of the soldiers came out, and the interpreter told him what we were there for. He said he wanted to thank us for not causing him anymore trouble. He was very good to us, and soon after this, the soldiers gave us some food.

Then we told the interpreter to tell the chief that we never wanted to fight, but we only wanted to lead our lives as we had been doing for many years. I said that we knew our past record was against us and that some of our people had brought the trouble on themselves and deserved the punishment they were getting, but we who did not want trouble felt that we did not deserve to be punished for the sins of someone else. Now we had decided there was nothing for us to do but to go with them.

I explained that we would have come in to the soldiers' camp before, but we were afraid of the Utes. They had always been our enemies, and we knew that they would welcome the chance to kill as many of us as they could. I asked him to send some of the soldiers with us to our camp. He said that he would do this. I asked him not to take any Utes to our camp. He said he knew he could trust us and would not send any of the Utes to our camp with us. He told us not to be afraid, as we would be well treated in the place we were to be sent.

The soldiers told the people that they must travel many miles to an army fort in New Mexico. Some captives came to the soldiers' camp carrying their possessions on their backs.

The Long Walk

The next morning we started on our long journey. There were about fifty of our people. Some of the soldiers went with us, but some of the others started in another direction. I asked Mother where they were going. She said they were going to hunt down some more of our people. The soldiers who were with us took one of the wagons and one of the big guns.

I was so interested in watching these things being drawn along by the horses and mules. I watched the wheels go around and around all day and for several days after this until we reached a place where we were to stay for a while. There, for the first time, I saw a white man's house. It was different from our hogans or the stone houses under the rocks that the ancestors of the Hopis (*Oozíís*) had built.

Grandfather said there would be little for me to do for some time. He told me to look around and see what there was of interest, as there were still things for me to learn about. We stayed at that place for some time. Every day, more and more of our people were brought in.

The soldiers said that some of our people were still fighting, and our war chief would not give up. Some of the people who were brought in were driven like sheep. They were not allowed to bring their horses, and their sheep had been killed. They were carrying heavy packs on their backs. These were the ones who had wanted to fight. Some of the others came in peaceably as we had done.

Grandfather told the ones who had complained that it was their own fault. He said they had not tried to control their young men, so the whole tribe must suffer.

As the days went by, the war chief and his band continued fighting. Our people who wanted peace hoped every day that the next party to be brought in would be the warriors. We were all very glad when they were at last captured. We all wanted to see how the war chief would act now that he was in the camp. The soldiers tried to treat these people well, but

After the captives reached the army fort in New Mexico, some of them were allowed to set up a camp several miles from the fort.

they were sullen and would not eat. They still had the spirit of war in their hearts. The old men talked to them, but they would not listen.[4]

We finally resumed our long walk, and, after many miles, the day came at last when we reached the place where we were to stay. The winter came very soon, and we had nothing to do but visit among ourselves. Grandfather talked to us more than he had been able to when he had his work to do.

For some time, everything went well. Then some of the people died. The old people said they could not stand the meat the white people gave us. It was bacon. They did not know how to make bread of the flour. Many of the people died during the winter, but most of them were the ones who would not try to learn how to cook the food they had to eat. We who were trying to be satisfied with our lot were well most of the time.

When spring came, some of the old people asked the soldiers to let them have some land to put in cornfields. The soldiers gave us some land a few miles from the fort, and we moved our camps there. Soon most of the people were busy putting in the corn and were contented.

There were still those among us who were trying to cause trouble, but they were too few to make much headway. Of course, we were not as happy as we would have been if we had been in our own land and had been free to do as we pleased. But there were many flowers as the summer came on, and Grandfather began to teach me about them. He showed me many plants that grew in our own country. I was very much interested in them.

We did not have many ceremonies, as the white doctor took care of us when we were not well. Grandfather said that we would be allowed to go back to our own country when all the people got the thought of war out of their hearts and tried to do as they should.

Our war chief spent most of his time making arrows. Some of the old men told him that if he would get the evil thought out of his heart, he would not need so many arrows. "You have heard what the white chief in Washington has said," one man told him. "If we promise not to make anymore raids on the people of the towns and the Indians of the villages, we will be allowed to return to our own land, and they will protect us against our enemies—the Apaches and Utes."

"We have heard all of this, but I do not believe it," the war chief replied. "They have made promises to us before, but they have not kept them. I am going to keep on making arrows."

4 The war chief was probably Barboncito, who was brought into Los Pinos, New Mexico, in August 1864.

One day my brother and I went down to the creek that was near our camp. We were searching for plants that I wanted to learn about. While we were looking around among the willows, we heard a terrible noise in the camp. We thought our people were fighting, but when we reached a place from which we could see, we saw that our old enemies, the Comanches, were making a raid on the people. We were frightened, and we lay down in the grass and watched the fight.

Soon we heard the bugle at the fort and saw many soldiers coming to help us. When the Comanches saw the soldiers coming, they started to run. Both the soldiers and our people followed them. When they came back, they said they had killed several of the Comanches, and several of our people had been killed.

We had a man in our camp who had been among us from the time he was a little boy. He was a Mexican who our people had stolen when they made one of their raids some years before. Not being one of our people, he was not afraid of the dead. He came into camp with the scalps of three of the Comanches tied to his belt. When our people saw them, they made much fuss. They told him that his actions would cause us all trouble, and he would have to bury the scalps and have himself cleansed of the blood, or else leave the camp. He buried the scalps, took a sweat bath, and had some prayers said before any of the people, except the medicine man, would go near him.

The soldiers buried our people who had been killed. One of our girls was missing. We knew that the Comanches had taken her, and some of the people wanted to go after her. But they decided it would be of no use to take the risk of going into the country of the enemy to try to fight. We had no guns or ammunition. We were not allowed to have anything to fight with. Also, the old men said it would not be right for the families of the ones who had been killed to go anywhere until the spirit of the dead had time to make the fourth circle. One of my father's brothers had been killed, so we had to stay at our hogan for four days.

On the sixth night after the battle, the girl who had been stolen came in just before dawn. She said that one of the women in the enemy's camp had cut the ropes with which she had been bound and gave her a horse to get away on. She rode for two nights and rested for a short time during the day. None of the enemy had followed her.

After four winters of this life, our war chief said that he would be willing to agree to the signing of the papers that the white chief at

After four years of captivity, the people were allowed to return to their homeland. These elders are prepared for a journey.

Washington wanted our people to sign. We were all so glad because now we would be allowed to go back to our own country. The time soon came when we at last started back over the road on which we had come.

The soldiers took us to the river we had crossed on our way there and helped us back across. They said we might need something to fight with because an Apache war party might attack us if we were not armed. They gave our men their spears and shields and some guns and ammunition. They also gave us food, clothing, and blankets. Then we were on our own.

When the captives returned home, their priority was to gather food for the winter. Even the young boys were taught to hunt.

Home

It did not seem long before we were in our own country, and we were very happy. Grandfather said we would have to start to work to get a supply of food. We began to gather various kinds of grass seeds. My brother and I were now old enough to work with the men, and they told us they would take us on their next hunting trip. We were very anxious for that time to come, but we must first work to gather as much food as we could.

Grandfather went out with me every day, and, as we gathered the seeds, he told me many things about the different plants—how they were used for food or medicine and how they must be gathered when they were to be used for medicine. He told me what chants they were used in. I grew more interested in them as the days went by.

We saw many of our people who had not gone with us when the soldiers had taken us prisoners. They said they had had it very hard at times while we were gone. We told them that it had not been so bad where we had been, but we were glad to be back again so that we could live our own lives as we wanted to live them. The old people said it would have been better to listen to the man who said that if we would go peaceably, we would have no trouble.

I now knew what war was and hoped I would never see anymore of it. Grandfather told the people that the way to avoid war was never to think of it. He said that we should get rid of all of our spears and shields, as they were implements of war and would bring thoughts of war. Now that we were at peace again, we should not have anything around to remind us of war. Many of the old men agreed with my grandfather, so we decided to bury the spears and shields in caves in the canyons.

Some of the white people came to a place we called Big Meadows. They told the people that they would have food and clothing for them there. A good many of us went in and received what they had to give us. Sometime after this, they called us in again and gave us some sheep. We would now be able to start another flock of sheep, and we were grateful to the chief at Washington.

The people who returned from the Long Walk had to rebuild their communities. Poles were used to build corrals and other structures.

We kept on gathering food, as we did not want to stay around Big Meadows. We wanted to make our own living. Grandfather said that we would lose our strength if we sat down and waited for the white people to feed us.

The Hunt

Soon the time came for the hunt, and I was anxious to go. Grandfather said that we must go through a ceremony on our way to the hunting grounds. He had shown me how to gather the pollen from certain plants that were used in the ceremony. I did as he instructed me, and put the pollen in a little buckskin bag. Now the time had come for it to be used.

A number of men gathered at our hogan for the early morning start. Before dawn of the next day, we were ready to leave. The morning was bright and cool. We could see snow on the tops of the higher mountains as the sun peeped over them. They changed from dark blue to red, and then to yellow and white. We had had much rain that year, and the bright yellow of the rabbit brush blossoms, the purple and white of the asters, and the gray of the sage against the rocks were beautiful.

We camped near the Ute River the first night. The next morning, as soon as it was light enough for us to see their tracks, we went out after our horses. The sun was just peeping over the red mesas when we resumed our journey. Soon we got to the bank of the river. There we stopped to perform the ceremony and say the prayer for the success of the hunt. We all stood there while my grandfather performed the ceremony.

He held some white shell, turquoise, jet, red stone, and abalone shell beads in his hand. He put some of the pollen from the little buckskin bag in his hand with the beads and said the prayer as he let the river wash his hands clean of the beads and pollen. The prayer was a prayer to the God of Speech and the God of the Hunt.

God of Speech, Chief of the Hunt,
Let the Big Deer Chief of the deer come to me;
Let the red stone arrow points go into his heart;
God of the Pollen, God of Life,
Let the big deer, the small deer, and all other kinds of deer come to me;
With my black bow, let me kill them;
Give me the heart of the big black deer;
I will kill them; I will kill them.

After he said the prayer, we mounted our horses and crossed the river. By this time, the sun was shining brightly. We could see the blue of the mountains to the north of us. The tops of the peaks were white with snow from a storm that had come through a few days before. The old men said the snow on the mountains would help us, as the deer would come down to the parks. The next day we reached the hunting grounds and made our camps.

At dawn the next morning, my grandfather repeated the prayer that he had said at the river. But this time he said "I will kill them" four times at the end of the prayer instead of twice as he had said before. This, I knew, meant that the prayer was ended. Then we ate our breakfast and started out to hunt.

Some of the men had guns, but most of us just had our bows. We went on foot to hunt, as we could not take the horses over the rougher places. We would have to follow the deer trails. The first day I saw many deer, but I could not get near enough to shoot them. When the evening came, I went in empty-handed, but some of the men came into camp carrying deer.

Grandfather said that he would go out with my brother and me the next day and teach us how to hunt. He had killed two deer, and since he could not carry both of them, he had left one of them hanging in a tree to be brought in the next day.

I was anxious to get a deer, so I was glad when morning came. We started out as soon as it was light enough for us to see to travel. Grandfather was very careful to take us a long distance around so that we could get to the opposite side of the park from which the wind was blowing. He said that the deer would now be feeding and we must be careful that they not smell us. Our moccasins made no noise, and we could walk silently if we were careful.

Soon we reached the timber. Near the park, several deer were feeding quietly. We crawled closer and closer to them until we were within shooting distance. Grandfather told us to take aim at the biggest deer nearest to us. We shot, and Grandfather and I each killed a deer. My brother was not successful. I was very much excited at killing my first deer, but I was sorry for my brother. By this time, some of the other men were shooting, and the deer began to run. My brother would have to wait until later to get his deer.

The next day he killed a deer, and I was very glad. I had no success that day, as the deer were now afraid. Two days later, I killed another one. By that time, we had all we could carry. We spent the next day stripping the meat from the bones and packing it in sacks to carry home with us.

Early the next morning we started for our hogans. When we got within a few miles of home, we stopped and camped for the night. Grandfather said that there we must clean ourselves of the blood of the hunt.

The sun was dipping toward the west when we reached the camp, but we needed to build a sweathouse before sunset. We quickly gathered cedar timbers and built the structure. Then we stripped the bark from the logs and put it all around the sides on the floor to lie on. We heated some stones and put them in the center of the sweathouse. When it was hot enough, three or four men at a time went in and stayed as long as they could. Then they came out to give some more of us our turn. When we were wet with perspiration, we came out and took a bath in cold water. Then we were cleansed of the blood and were ready to return to our hogans.

It was late by the time everyone was through bathing. We ate our supper and slept the rest of the night.

We reached our home early the next day. The women started drying the meat we had brought in. We all rejoiced, as there would be enough meat to last us through the winter. For another year, we would have peace.

I told my grandfather I was glad that we had all we needed. He said I should not fear the future. "You must live today and keep your thoughts in the path of light. Everything will come out all right. You must always think that the next year of your life will be more happy and peaceful than the year before, and must try to make it come true."

When they had ample provisions in store for the winter, the people were at peace and could enjoy each other's company.

Marriage

When spring came, my people said it was time for me to be married. I told them I did not want to live too far away from them, as I wanted my grandfather to teach me more about the plants and ceremonies. They said they would be glad to have me stay near them. At a nearby hogan was a girl of marriageable age. She was a member of a clan into which I could marry. My grandfather and uncle went there to ask for the girl. When they came back, they had made all the arrangements for our wedding. It would be in a month.

The young women had their own social circles. These women are wearing velveteen blouses, multilayered skirts of calico, and beads of turquoise, white shell, and coral.

I did not know whether I was going to like being away from my mother or not. I told her this, and she said that I should not have such thoughts. "You are a strong man, my son, and you must live your life as you were meant to live it. You will be happy if you treat your wife right. I know the girl, and she is a good person. I am glad she lives so close to us. I can see you almost every day. You must work and make a cornfield of your own. You will still have your sheep here in our flock. I will take care of them."

By this time, the number of sheep that we had was almost as large as it had been before we were taken away from our country. My grandfather, being a medicine man, had received many of them for his services, and I had received many as payment for gathering medicines for him. Some of the people who were not taken prisoners gathered the sheep they could find that belonged to those of us who had been taken away, and we were given some of those as well.

The wedding day soon came, and we went to the hogan where I was to live from then on. After the wedding was over and my wife and I were alone, I looked at her and decided that she was good looking. I thought I was lucky to have a wife like her. She was very quiet, and at first she would not talk to me very much. As the days went by, we became happy. Her family were very good people, and I got along well with them. I had known them for a long time before I was married. Some of the men had gone on the hunting trip with us.

My wife asked me to tell her about the white people and the war. I told her the war was not a pleasant subject, and we must not talk about it too much. I did describe to her the foods that we had and the clothing of the white men.

My wife had a good many sheep, as her family had not gone with us when we were taken away by the white people. The deer were plentiful again that year, and we returned with meat enough for the winter. We were glad that we would not have to kill any of our sheep until the next summer, as we wanted them to multiply.

A Raid

The women had woven many blankets through the summer, as we planned to go to the Zuni villages on a trading trip after the hunt was over. We needed salt and could get it from the salt lakes near Zuni. We left two strong men and several old men and boys to guard the camps.

When we were all ready to start, one of the old men, who was a peace chanter, said the prayer for success of the journey, and then we started on our way. A few miles out on our trail, we came to a shrine. It was a pile of stones with medicine plants and boughs of cedar in between them. Here we stopped to say a prayer and add more stones and plants to it.

After several days, we reached our destination. The Zunis were friendly and seemed pleased to see us. They were glad to trade us beads, turquoise, and dried peaches for our blankets and buckskins. We stayed with them several days, trading and watching a ceremony that they were having. I was glad to see their beautiful ceremony, and I now realized what a terrible thing our people had done when they stole the sheep and girls that started the war.

This was my first trading trip, and I now had a chance to see how it was all the fault of our own people when they had trouble with the people of the villages. I had not seen many of the villages, but Grandfather said they were very much alike in their friendliness toward us.

We finished trading and went to the salt lake to get the salt. Then we started on our way back to the hogans. We camped a little way from our hogans to say our prayers and take a sweat bath before returning home after a long journey.

At dawn the next morning, when we young men went out to get our horses, we found a pinto horse dead. We knew that it was not one of ours. We looked at him and decided that he was a Ute horse. He had a Navajo arrow in his side. By this, we knew that there had been a raid.

We hurried the horses back to the camp and told the old men what we had found. They said there had been a raid and we must hurry to the hogans. We soon reached the first hogans. There we found all of the old men and several of the older boys dead, but the two strong men who had been left at the place were not among them. Then we saw the tracks of the sheep and people going toward the timber nearby. We followed them and found one of the men dead.

We started looking for the other man and soon found his mutilated body with his left arm lying across it. This they had left there out of respect for him. The bow was by his side, but he had no bow guard, and his wrist had been cut by the bowstring until there was no flesh left on it. By his side was a woman with a quiver of arrows. We knew by his arm how hard he had fought. Of course, we could do nothing with the bodies; in war we must leave them where they fall. The women, children, and sheep were all gone.

It looked as though it was going to snow. The old men began to pray for a storm. When we started on the pursuit, the trail of the people and sheep was fresh and we knew the Utes were not very far ahead of us. We traveled fast. The Utes did not see us coming, as the timber was thick. They could not hear us, as the sheep and the children were making so much noise because they were so frightened. We saw the Utes start to drive the women and children down the trail off the mountain. Here we dismounted and slipped down each side of the trail.

There was a little wash and much brush on each side of the trail. It began to snow, and the man who was leading the Utes put his buffalo robe up over his head and one eye. We could see that four of the Utes had four girls from our hogans behind them on their horses. The leader had a girl on behind him.

We opened fire on the Utes, but we had to be careful not to shoot our own girls. The Utes were so taken by surprise that they did not fight much, but drove the women, children, and sheep all the faster. They did not know how many of us they had to fight, so they rushed on, trying to get away. Soon they had to let the sheep go. They killed some of the older women and some of the babies.

After we drove them for several miles, they decided to leave the women and children. We were unable to recover the food they had stolen, but they did not get very much. We knew we were not strong enough to fight them, so we had to let the stolen girls go. We took the women and children who had been released to the nearest hogan and asked the Navajo people who lived there for help.

Now I knew what a Ute raid could be. If we had not surprised them, we would have lost all of our women and children, and they would have made raids on as many hogans as they could find. The man who had fought so hard was my father's brother. We were all very sad over the loss of the girls and the people who had been killed.

We were all sitting around our hogans, waiting for the four days of mourning to go by. We could do nothing but wait for the spirits to make the four circles before they were ready to go on their way to the other

Three girls were captured by the Utes and taken across the San Juan River to the north. One of the captured girls quickly escaped. This girl is standing in the shade of a summer hogan.

land. A number of us were gathered at one hogan, as now we must guard them for fear that the Utes might come back.

Just at dawn of the second day after the raid, one of the captured girls came in. She said that she had gotten away the first night out while the Utes were asleep and had traveled all of the rest of the night. She heard no one pursuing her, but she was very afraid. During the day, she hid in the rocks. Throughout the night she ran, so she was very tired. The other girls had not succeeded in escaping.

After the four days were over, the women of the hogans on which the raids had been made told us about it. They said that Warrior Girl (*Naadlį' Naazbaa',* "Warrior Girl Went on a Raid"), one of the girls who had been stolen, was ill. She was beautiful and much loved, so every effort had to be made to make her well again. The people called in a medicine man to go into a trance to tell them what the cause of the illness was. He said that since the girl had some evil thoughts the God of Peace had caused it. A peace chant must be given to dispel this evil. So her family started to prepare for a chant to be given as soon as we returned from Zuni.

The family did not have some of the medicine plants to be used in the chant, so they sent two of the boys to the mouth of the Mancos River, about one hundred miles away, to gather the medicine. They said they knew it was near Ute country, but they did not think the Utes would bother them since they had not made a raid in a long time. They warned the boys to be careful and to gather the plants near the rocks, if possible, so they would not make too many tracks, as the Utes might kill two boys alone if they found them.

The boys returned safely, and the people made the rest of the preparations for the chant. Almost all of the bows and guns and all of the bow guards were carried out of the camp and hidden in the rocks. They only kept two guns and a few bows with which to kill rabbits and prairie dogs for food, as in a peace chant there must be nothing around that pertains to war. They were praying for peace, and they had to believe the prayers would be answered.

All of the preparations were finished, and everything was going well until just before dawn of the day of the raid. One of the old men who had kept his bow in the hogan woke the people in the hogan with him and told them something was going to happen. "My bow string keeps singing and will not let me sleep," he said. "We must see what the matter is." He told one of the boys to call all of the people from their hogans. The people all ran to the hogan of the old man. Just then, the first streak of dawn came, and with it, the Utes rode up to one of the hogans and started the raid.

The old man told the two strong men who had stayed in the camp to take the women, children, and sheep out into the timber in back of the hogans. The old men and boys stayed in the camp to try to save as much food as they could, but it was no use. Soon they were all killed, as they only had a few bows with which to fight. The Utes then went into the timber after the women and children.

They soon killed one of the men, as he only had a few cartridges and arrows. The other man soon used up all of his cartridges, and he began to shoot his bow. His wife stood by him and handed him the arrows as he shot them. When his wrist was so torn by the bowstring that he could not fight any longer, the Utes killed him and mutilated his body. They put his left arm out so the people could see how hard he had fought.

A little boy and girl who had been herding sheep then said that they had seen two of the Utes the day before the raid. They saw two men on some rocks a distance away who were wearing red blankets. At first, they were frightened, as they thought it was strange for a Navajo to be wearing a red blanket. They watched the men for some time but did not feel threatened, as they did not come near them and soon went in the other direction. They thought they were Navajos from some other hogan and that they must have gotten their red blankets from the white people. By the time evening came, the children took the sheep to the hogan and forgot all about seeing the men.

The people worried about the captured girls. Since we had very little ammunition and few guns, we knew it would be of no use for us to go up into the Ute country to try to rescue them. We would all be killed.

The old people said we must try to forget our troubles, so we talked no more of the raid and just went on living our lives as before.

We had much snow that winter. We had to work very hard cutting the tops of the trees down to feed our sheep until the snow was gone again. Then the time for planting of the fields came again and we went on working.

Escape

It was almost the middle of summer again. One morning, the sun was just peeping through the curtains of dawn and we were getting ready to go to the fields when Warrior Girl came into the hogan where we were. We were all so glad to see her. Her moccasins were worn out, her feet were bleeding, her clothes were torn to shreds, she was almost starved, and she was exhausted. She was a sad sight.

The women began cooking something for her to eat while one of the old men brewed some plants from his medicine bag. He began to chant a prayer for her recovery. As soon as the medicine was brewed, she was given some to drink, and her face and the upper part of her body were bathed in it. Soon she was rested enough to eat and was given food. Then the women made a soft pallet of sheepskins and robes for her. She quickly fell asleep. Some of the elders said she would be able to tell us her story by the time the sun was gone that night.

We went on with our work throughout the day. We were looking forward to the evening when we could hear the story, but no one talked about it. We were all very quiet all day. When we reached the hogan in the evening, Warrior Girl was still resting, but when our supper was ready, she came, took a place among us, and ate. She said she was well and would tell us her story.

When everything was finished for the night, many people from the nearby hogans who had heard of her return joined us. We sat in front of the hogan. The night was clear, and the stars were very bright.

Warrior Girl began her story. She said it was her fault that this trouble had come to her and the rest of her people. She had caused the death of her father and mother, as her father was the one who had fought so hard to save the people, and her mother had been killed while she stood by him, handing him the arrows. She had seen them shot down.

> I was the one who had the evil thoughts that started the whole thing. I went against the rules of our people and was afraid when the old medicine man went into the trance to tell me why I was ill. I was afraid he would know what the thoughts in my mind had

After nearly a year in captivity by the Utes, one of the other girls escaped and returned home. Wolfkiller recounted her story of suffering and daring. These young people are wearing fine handwoven robes.

been. He said that I needed a peace chant to clear my thoughts. He was right, as my cousin, Gray One (*Báhí*), and I had had a talk about one of the young men who would soon be wanting a wife, and we both hoped we would be the one his people would choose for him.

This, in itself, was an evil thought, as we knew that we were not the ones to say whom we should marry. I thought a good deal about it, and I grew to hate Gray One, although she was my cousin. I hoped something would happen to her. I was so jealous of her. I do not know what her thoughts were toward me, but we have both paid.

She is dead, and I have suffered almost more than I could bear at times. She did not suffer as long as I did, so I think she must have been better than me.

The Utes captured Gray One, Shore Clan Girl (*At'ééd Tábąąhí*), and me and took us to their camps up near the Black Mountain. They made us work for them day after day. If we were not strong enough to carry their wood, they whipped us with buckskin whips until our backs bled. Then some of the men decided they wanted us for their wives. We hated them, but there was nothing we could do. Shore Clan Girl did not fight back, so she was treated better than Gray One and I were treated.

Soon the wives of the men who had taken us for their wives grew jealous of us and said that we would be taken farther away from our people. They predicted that when summer came again, the men would grow tired of us and would sell us to the Mexicans as slaves.

Gray One cried most of the time from then until it began to get warm again. When the Utes began to prepare to go to their summer camps, she told the wife of the man who had taken her as his wife that she was not going with them and that she was going to try to escape. The Ute woman encouraged her to go.

One night, just before the move, Gray One slipped out in the night and started for home. The next morning the Utes laughed when they found she was not there. They said she would not be able to cross the river when she got to it, so they could follow her and easily recapture her.

They did not start after her until the sun was dipping toward the west. Then several of them started the chase. When they came back that night, she was not with them, and they were very angry. They said they had gotten near her as she stood on the bank of the river and had laughed at her and called to her to come back. They thought she would be afraid to go into the water, but after a little while, she plunged in. She could not swim and was carried down the river.

That night they bound my hands and feet. They did not bind Shore Clan Girl, as she was contented, but they were afraid that I would try to escape like Gray One had. From that time on, they guarded me and kept me bound at night. I was the wife of the chief's son, so I was taken to the summer camps. I grieved for Gray One, but I knew she was not having the punishment I was having, and I was glad for her. I knew her death was my fault, and I worried about this and could not sleep.

The Utes told me that the way they had found our camp was by following the tracks of the boys who had been sent out after the medicine for the chant that was to have been given for me. They said that some of them were out hunting horses, and they saw the boys' tracks. When they told the people in the camps about them, the chief said, 'That will be an easy way to find the Navajos, and it is about time we made a raid on them. It has been a long time since we have raided them. They are going to have a big chant of some kind, so they will be busy and have much food in the hogan. When the chant is being held, they will not be thinking of anything else, so we can surprise them and get some slaves and much food to carry us through the winter. It must be a big chant, or they would not have come so far for the medicine plants for it.'

When I heard this, I knew that I was to blame for all of the trouble, and I had that to worry about. I was afraid that I would be sold to the Mexicans and would never see my people again. I wished many times that I had gone with Gray One. She was at least safe from her own thoughts.

As the days went by, life and my own thoughts grew harder and harder to bear until I told the wife of the man who was also my husband that I would try to go home if she would help me. I knew she was jealous of me and would be glad to be rid of me. She also felt sorry for me since I was so unhappy. When I told her I wanted to try to go, she said she would cut the ropes with which I was bound and let me go that night.

When everyone was asleep, the woman slipped up to my bed and cut the ropes. She gave me a bag of dried meat and some bread to carry with me. I stole quietly out of the camp. I was afraid the dogs might bark, but they did not hear me. As soon as I was safely away from the camp, I began to run. I ran all the rest of the night, but when the sun came again, I hid and waited for the day to go by. I saw no one all day. I did not sleep, as I feared they might find me if I should go to sleep. By the time the dark had come again, I was rested enough to go on.

I ate a little food and started on again. I could not tell just where I was, but I watched the stars and knew I was going in the right direction. When it was light enough for me to see, I looked for the mountains I had to pass. When I started on again, I knew where I was going and where the river was that I would have to cross.

The clouds began to come up, and I was afraid that it would rain. I came on as fast as I could. The clouds grew darker and darker as the night went by. It began to rain just before the dawn came, but by this time I had crossed a small river. I still had the big river to cross, and it began to rain harder in the mountains at its head. I went on until after the sun came out, and then I hid again. I saw no one following me.

I knew the Utes thought I could not cross the river and that I would be too tired to continue. Since they had horses to follow me, they did not hurry. I had to sleep that day, as I was so tired. The rain continued almost all day. I felt better when I started again, but water was running everywhere from the rain. The rain had not stopped, but it was lighter than it had been during the day. I went to the top of a hill to see if I could hear anyone, and from there I saw a campfire. I then knew they were following me, so I ran as fast as I could. The mud was getting bad, so it became harder and harder to travel.

By the time I at last reached the river, the sun had come out. I saw the Utes, but they were still some distance away. The river was running high, and it was very muddy. I dragged a cottonwood log up to its edge just as the Utes came up on the bank above. They stood there watching me and laughing, thinking that I would be afraid to cross. I was relieved to see only five of them, and I reasoned that they probably would not follow me far into our country on the other side of the river with such a small group. After staring at the water for a while, I pushed the log into the water and started in after it. The Utes stopped laughing and watched me as I crossed the river.

When I was safely across, they again started after me, but they had trouble with their horses. I reached a place where I could climb a hill that I knew they could not get their horses up. I hid in the rocks to watch them, and I saw they were hunting my tracks. Then I came on as far as I could and hid again. I was so tired that I could not go any farther, and I was compelled to rest and eat a little food.

By this time, my food was almost gone, but I was too tired to eat much anyway. I lay down and prayed that they would not find me. After resting awhile, I continued. I hoped to find a hogan of some of my people, but did not see any. At times, I had to rest. Then the night came again, and I came on slowly as long as I could walk. I saw no more of the Utes, so I rested all day. Then, when the night came again, I ate a little more food and continued. Since I was no longer in the rocks, I knew I must be careful.

When the dawn came again, I hid in a wash and rested all day. I had only one piece of bread left, but I did find some water to drink. When the sun went down, I ate my last piece of bread and waited for night. When it came, I started on and traveled all last night.

I was so glad to see the hogan this morning. I was almost ready to give up, but I kept coming. Now that I am safe, nothing else matters.

Warrior Girl finished her story. For a while, no one spoke. We were all so sorry for her. Then one of the old men said, "My daughter, you have suffered for your evil thought, and now you must not think anything more about it. You know that the path of evil thought leads you nowhere but into the dark, and now that you have found yourself, you will be the better for this wandering. It will make you stronger, and when you have your own children, you can tell them your story and it will make them afraid to do the things they know are not right. So from this day on, you must go with peace in your heart. We will have a peace chant, though, to get your mind clear of all you have gone through."

A few days after this we made preparations for the chant. I was sent out to get the medicine for it. We still had the medicine the boys had gotten near the Ute country the year before, so we did not need to go there again. The chant lasted five days. When it was finished, Warrior Girl was much better. We said no more about her troubles.

Drought

Three more years went by before we had anymore trouble. Then the rain did not come in the summer but the wind blew very hard. Our corn did not grow very well, as it needed the rain. The old people said, "We must not talk much about the weather, for we have enough food to last us a year, anyway, and this is much better than it had been at times in the past."

The earth still had a little moisture in it, and we harvested a small amount of corn. We also gathered grass seeds and dug potatoes when we could find them in the canyons. We went on a hunt, but did not get as many deer as we had the year before. Grandfather said we must not complain, as we were much better off than the people of earlier years had been. We still had the sheep, and, while they were not fat, they were still living. They still had a few weeds and greasewood to eat.

The winter came, but there was no snow. The next summer there was no rain. Our horses began to die, and we had to gather food anywhere we could find it. I said that I thought it was terrible. Grandfather told me not to talk about it or think about it. "We will not starve," he said, as someone had told him that the people at the Big Meadows would give us food when we needed it. "We are not suffering so much yet," he added.

When the drought came and the crops would not grow, Wolfkiller's family relied on their livestock for sustenance.

Wool and pelts provided the Navajos with clothing and goods that could be used to trade for other essentials.

When another winter came, we had to go to the white people for food. Many of our sheep and almost all of our horses died, but Grandfather was still optimistic. "We are still better off than the people have been at times in the past, as there was now some place to get food from. Back then there was no food anywhere."

We still kept on praying for rain and trying to be happy. Another winter went by with no snow.

When the spring came, we had a little rain and planted some corn in the damp places. The summer brought a little more rain. With our corn and what food we could gather, we knew we would be able to go on, and the few sheep we had left would grow fat again. We still had a few horses left and were happy.

When the middle of summer came, some of the old men said, "We need some buckskins for medicine bags and thongs for ceremonies. Now would be a good time to get them, as there is now water everywhere for the deer to drink." We planned a hunt for the deer.

We got as many men together as we could and started for the mountains to the north of us. When we came to the first journey shrine, we performed our ceremony for the success of the hunting trip. Then we went on. When we came to the river, we again performed the ceremony of the hunt, but we did not pray for the red arrow point to go into the heart of the deer. This time we prayed that the deer would come to us.

When we reached the mountains, we went to all of the water holes to which deer tracks led and to the places where the water was salty. There the deer would come to lick the white minerals around the edge. Grandfather explained that the deer had to have this mineral. After we surveyed all the places where the deer could drink, we saw that there were not many of them.

Then we separated in parties. Each group was assigned to guard a water hole and let the deer drink for several days. The salty water holes were left unguarded. We were on guard night and day. For two days, we did not see any deer. We knew they would not come near us at first, as they would smell the smoke from our fires and would hear us chanting.

We chanted a part of each day and each night. On the third day, we saw several deer on the hills above us. They came and looked at us, and then ran away. The old men said we would not have to wait very long this year, as the grass was very dry and the deer would be very thirsty soon with no water to drink except the salty water.

The next day they came nearer, but they were still so much afraid of us that they ran away. They could not run very fast, though. "We will not have to wait much longer," the old men said. "They are very thirsty now." That night they tried again to come to water, but were still afraid of us. It was a bright night, and they stood around on the hills. We could see them silhouetted with their heads up and their horns back. The old men said they were still able to run.

The next morning at dawn, they again tried to come to the water and got very close to us. The old men said we would be able to catch them the next day. All that day they stood around us on the hills with not enough strength to throw their heads back. That night they were very near us, but we sat around the water so they could not get to it. At dawn the next morning, we moved away a short distance and let them come in to drink. They rushed in as soon as we were away, and were so thirsty that they fell over each other. I thought they never would get enough water, but they soon started away slowly. They were so full of water that they could not run.

Then we all went after them—two or three men to each deer. We selected the biggest ones. When they saw us coming, they tried to run, but we could catch them easily. We caught them and held their noses so they could not breathe.

When they were dead, we chanted our prayers. Then we skinned them and cut off their horns and toes. The toes and shoulder blades were to be used to make rattles, the horns to make awls, and the other things for the medicine bags. Then we buried the carcasses, and our work was done. We had four deer. The rest of them we did not bother. According to our ceremonial law, we could not eat the meat from a deer killed this way.

As we finished our ceremonies at the water hole, we started for our hogans. We could not eat until we were some distance from the water and all of the parties who were at the different water holes were back together.

The sun was dipping far to the west when we reached the meeting place. Some of the other parties were ahead of us. They had some deer, too. Soon after we reached that place, the rest of the parties came in. There we camped for the night. We could eat now, and I was glad, as I was very hungry. On the way home, we had to perform our cleansing ceremonies in the sweat house, as we always did a few miles from our hogans.

We were very busy for some days making medicine bags, rattles, awls, and other things for the medicine bags.

Soon after this, harvest time came. We had more corn that year than we had had for the previous two years, and we were happy again. When the winter came, there was much snow and we could not do very much traveling around. We were glad to see the snow again after the dry years, and I knew why the old people said we must not complain about anything.

A Necessary Evil

Although the old people did not like to talk about unpleasant things of the past, I still had the question on my mind about why the people had thought it was all right to go out and make war on the Pueblos. I knew that Grandfather would not tell me stories of war or of many other things while the snakes and lightning were awake, but now that it was winter, I decided to ask him my question.

That night I went to my mother's hogan. Everyone was sitting around the fire talking when I went in. I looked at my grandfather and thought of the years gone by when he had told me stories. He did not look much older now than he had looked then. I told him what I was thinking about him.

"My grandson," he said, "my thoughts are still in the path of light, and the path of light never grows old. It is when people think evil thoughts that they grow old and helpless. We must not think of growing old, and, if we live as we should live, we will not grow old. The time will come for all of us to go to the other land, and when it comes, we must be ready to go. As I have told you, we must live this life right if we want to be happy in the other land. If we go there with the right thoughts in our minds, we will not suffer anymore. But if we go with evil thoughts, we will have to be punished for them. We still have a chance, though. If we try to get our thoughts in the right path, we will have a peaceful life, but if we still keep thinking of evil things, we will have to die again and go to a land that is not beautiful. From that land, we will still have a chance to come back to the land of peace. But if we persist in thinking evil, we will have to go to a land that is all dark where there is no sunlight, where it is always night, and there are no flowers or trees. If we go to this land, there we will stay forever. Then we will be lost. We hope there are not many people in the dark land."

No one spoke for a while. We were thinking of what Grandfather had just said. Then I asked him about the raids. "My grandson," he replied, "I thought you had forgotten all about that. You have not said anything about it for a long time. I will tell you about it, as I think you should know why we have our marriage law."

The houses called Keet Seel were built by a tribe from Navajo Mountain, Wolfkiller said.

Many years ago, just after we came to the place where we now live, a drought came to the land. The winters and summers went by without snow or rain until several years had passed. The people who were in the houses under the rocks in Canyon de Chelly (*tséyi'ítso*, "Big Canyon") were compelled to move from their homes. A few of them came to live among our people. The rest of them went to the foot of the White Reed Mountains where there was still a little moisture in the ground. There they built more houses.

Still the rain did not come, and the people kept on struggling to live. The people who lived in houses stayed in one place for a while but eventually had to move on. Our people did not live in houses, so it was easier for them to move from place to place.

At the same time, another tribe lived under the high mesa above the Mancos River (*tó nts'ósíkooh*). These people had built their houses under the cliffs, as they were afraid of other tribes who made raids on them from time to time. With only one side to watch and one trail to get into the houses, they were safer than they would have been if they had lived out in the valleys.

They had lived in these houses for many years, but when the drought came, they were compelled to move. The people from the high mesas moved toward the sunset at the same time that the people from Canyon de Chelly were moving from place to place. Both tribes built houses on the flats.

They no longer feared war, as they had nothing that their enemies would want. They had very little food and were too busy hunting for food enough to keep life in their bodies to do any weaving. The enemies were also busy hunting food.

The rain came again, but for some time there was still no war. By this time, the people from Canyon de Chelly were living in villages in the valleys, and the people from the mesa were living at the foot of Navajo Mountain (*naatsis'áán*) . Then came another period of war. The people from the valleys and the people from Navajo Mountain moved into the canyon that we call Tsegi (*tséyi*), where there were cliffs under which to build their houses. The people from Canyon de Chelly built the houses we call Betatakin (*bitát'ahkin*), and the people from Navajo Mountain built the houses we call Keet Seel (*kits'iil*). You have seen the houses, my grandson.

Although two different tribes lived in the canyon, they did not mingle with one another much, as they spoke different languages. Soon the tribes grew larger, and they built houses in some of the branch canyons. The land was very fertile, and the canyon had several lakes in it.

Everything went well for some time, but then another drought came. The lakes began to dry up, the corn did not grow very well, and the people grew weaker. Then the rain came again, but very soon after this, the wind began to blow. It blew for many days, harder and harder until even the trees went down before it. Then a great hailstorm came. By this time, these people were very weak. They were trying to survive, but they had married into their own families and many of them were blind, deaf, or hunchbacked. They were getting too weak to fight for their existence.

Then a time came when snakes were moving everywhere. The people from the different houses at last came together, but by this time, very few of them were left. They concluded that the canyon was bewitched, so they decided to move.

Wolfkiller told the history of the canyon tribes, who joined together and built pueblo villages.

During this time, our people had been moving around the country from place to place, but they were near the Tsegi Canyon when those people came out. Our people had visited them from time to time while they lived in the canyon, as some of our people were related to them through the people who had joined them at the time of the great drought. Our people had not been to visit them for some time, as they were too busy making a living. When our people saw how weak the canyon people were, they were shocked. Some of our old men said they were growing weaker because they needed new blood and had lived too long by themselves.

Our people decided to pass a law that anyone who married into his own family would be killed. Some of the old men asked how they could avoid marrying in their own family, as there were only a few of our people left. Many had died while the struggle for life was going on. Then the people decided to go out and steal girls from different tribes to save the life of our tribe.

After the two canyon tribes joined, they began to get stronger. After they came out of the Tsegi, they moved to the top of the Black Mountain, where they built some houses and lived for a while. Then they moved to the place called Oraibi (*oozéí*) where they now live.

Our people began sending out parties of men to steal girls from the Pueblos, and our tribe grew stronger. Now, my grandson, you know what we mean when we say that at one time it was all right for us to make raids on the Pueblos.

My grandson, you now have your question answered. Our people were many years learning that to live and be strong, we must not live too much by ourselves. Our people have had some lessons in the past that made them understand this.

You can learn something from the trees about things like this. Have you never noticed that when a tree grows by itself on a point where the wind sweeps the earth from its roots, it becomes smaller and smaller? Then there are the trees that grow in places where new soil is blown in from among other plants and trees. Trees growing in places like that grow stronger and stronger.

Your father's clan is the clan that joined us when the people came out of Canyon de Chelly at the time of the great drought. They brought with them our night chant. That is why it is their chant. It does not belong to the rest of us.

That night I stayed at my mother's hogan, as it was snowing very hard. I thought a great deal about what my grandfather had said that evening and years earlier when the spirit of war had come into our land. We now had many clans and did not need new blood to save the life of the tribe. I hoped the time would never come again when we would go back to our old ways.

Keeping the Faith

When spring came again and the eagles were building their nests, some of the old men said they needed feathers for their medicine bags. They had made some new rattles and other ceremonial things and replaced the thongs on their old rattles, but they needed more feathers for their prayer sticks and wands. They decided to go out and catch some eagles.

The people used natural materials for ceremonial objects and other material goods. This craftsman is making moccasins of buckskin and sinew.

Grandfather had explained to me how they caught the eagles to get the feathers. The eagles fight hard when they are caught, but must not be killed. He said they are very powerful, and the man who catches them must be strong enough to hold them. I was now looking forward to the time when the nesting of the eagles would come, as I wanted to see how it was done.

Several of us went on a hunt to catch three or four rabbits that would be used as decoys to catch the eagles. We were instructed not to wound the rabbits. In some brush, we saw several rabbits. We encircled the brush and kept the rabbits running all day until they were tired and we could catch them. By the time that we returned to our hogans, the sun was almost down. We took some string and tied one hind leg of each of the rabbits to a post of the hogan, to be kept there for a few days until they were a little tamer. For the first three or four days, they were too afraid to eat or drink, but after they learned that we would not hurt them, they ran around the hogan.

Some of us went out to ride among the higher rocks to look for eagle nests. We found two of them and returned for the only man in the area who knew how to catch eagles and was strong enough to hold them.

When we went to catch the eagles, some of the older men went with us. Before we left the hogan, we prayed and chanted, and then did it again when we reached the foot of the rocks on top of which was one of the eagle nests. At the base of some bushes, we cleared the brush and dug a pit large enough for a man to stand in. On top of the pit, we placed sticks spaced a little distance apart. Then we piled the brush on top of the sticks.

By this time evening had come. We moved some distance away to camp for the night. After we finished our supper, we chanted and said some prayers for the success of the catching of the eagles. Then we lay down in our robes to sleep awhile and wait for morning.

Just before dawn, we went to the pit with the man who was to catch the eagles. When he and the rabbits were in the pit and the brush was put back over it, we returned to our camp to wait. Soon after this the dawn came. The day was bright and beautiful, and the heavens were all red and yellow when the sun came over the mountains.

The eagles began to circle around the rock on which their nest was built. They seemed to float, not moving their wings. They were hunting food for their children. At first, they flew very high. Then they gradually began to fly lower. We slipped to the top of a rock from which we could see the pit. We lay very quiet. Soon we saw one of the rabbits run out of the pit and hop around in the weeds nearby. Then he went back into the pit. I knew the eagle-catcher in the pit was drawing him back. After a time, we knew that the eagle had seen the rabbit, as he began to circle around over the pit. Then the eagle-catcher let two rabbits come out of the pit. The eagle came a little nearer each time, but he did not swoop down for the rabbit. At last, in almost the middle of the day, he darted down. The man pulled the rabbit back into the pit. The eagle lit on the brush. There the eagle-catcher caught him and pulled him into the pit.

I ran to the pit to watch the ceremony of the taking of the feathers. The eagle fought very hard, but he could not get away. The eagle-catcher put a cloth over his head. Then he sprinkled pollen through the feathers as he chanted. He then pulled some feathers from the breast, and some small feathers from each wing, and several from his tail. Then he released the eagle and came out of the pit. His hands were bleeding, and he had several scratches on his face that were bleeding very badly, but he did not seem to mind the wounds.

We went to the camp where the sweathouse was ready for the eagle-catcher to take a bath. As soon as he had bathed, one of the medicine men bathed his wounds and the upper part of his body in some herbs that he had brewed for this purpose. Then we prayed and chanted for the eagle-catcher to be healed.

By this time, it was almost evening again. We ate our supper and went to sleep, as we must be up early again the next morning to catch the other eagle. We must have the feathers from both the male and the female.

The next day we performed the same ceremony. It was nearing the middle of the afternoon before the other eagle came down after the rabbits, so it was almost dark before we were through with the ceremony for the healing of the wounds. The next day we moved to another eagle nest, which was some distance away. There we performed the ceremony over again. By the time the last eagle was caught, the eagle-catcher's hands were badly cut, but he said he did not mind it. The next day we went back to our hogans.

At sunrise the next morning, the medicine man sprinkled pollen over the eagle feathers and said some prayers as they bound the feathers and put them into the medicine bags to be used later. Then the ceremony was complete.

Soon after this, it was time to plant the corn again. Grandfather said that this year we would have a ceremony the day the planting began to ensure a good crop. He said that we were beginning to lose some of our ceremonies, and that is why the worms had cut down some of our corn the year before. The other old men agreed with him.

Grandfather sent me out to get some plants for the ceremony. At dawn, on the day we were to start planting, the plants I had gathered were ground up with some small particles of moonstones and some prayers were said. Then the plants and stones were sprinkled through the seed corn while we chanted. We said some prayers, asking the heavens to send us rain, the Mother Earth to send the plants forth, strong and healthy, and the earth and the heavens to let them grow and ripen.

We then planted a few grains of corn. When the ceremony was over, we went back to the hogan for our breakfast. Then we started our planting in earnest.

We had a wonderful crop of corn that year. Grandfather said we must pray for help when we need it and we would always get it.

The Coyote Path

Just before the time of the harvest, I was out hunting my horses when Grandfather rode up. He said that some people from the top of the mountain had come and asked him to prepare a medicine chant. They had gone back home that morning with his medicine bag, and he had promised them that he would leave on the fourth day. He asked me to gather certain plants for him and to accompany him to the ceremony. I said that I would.

After I found my horses and took them in, I went out to gather the plants. It took me three days to find all of them.

We started our journey early on the day that Grandfather had promised to leave. After we had ridden only a short way, a coyote crossed our trail. He came from the north of the trail and crossed it diagonally. Grandfather asked me to watch very carefully to see if any more coyotes crossed in front of us. We rode along for some distance before we saw any more of them, and then we saw another one cross our trail. This time he came from south of the trail and crossed diagonally, going toward the north. Grandfather began to look worried, but rode along quietly.

I continued to watch the trail ahead very carefully. We had not gone far before another coyote crossed our trail a short distance ahead. This one also came from the north of the trail and went diagonally across toward the south.

Grandfather immediately stopped and turned back toward our hogan. He did not say a word until we had passed the place where the first coyote had crossed our trail.

After a short distance, he said, "My grandson, you must watch the trail ahead. No matter where you are going, you must never go on after three coyotes have crossed your trail. If they go diagonally across, their tracks are like a streak of lightning, and it is a warning to us that there will be trouble ahead. Now we must wait four more days before we can go to perform the ceremony. We must go to our hogans and stay there until the four days have passed. Then we can go again."

After the four days, we went to the hogan to perform the ceremony. When we reached it, we explained to the people there why we had not come before. They said they knew something had happened to stop us and were glad we had not come before. We learned that we could not have performed the ceremony when it was originally planned because one of the old people of their family had died five days earlier.

The next morning the sacred fire was built and the ceremony began. The fire must be kept burning until the end of the ceremony, which lasted nine days.

A short time after this, Grandfather came to me early one morning and said he had had a bad dream the night before. His brother, who had died many years before, had come to him.

> He did not say anything, but just stood and looked at me. He was dressed as I had seen him once before in a costume that was not supposed to be used except in a ceremony, and then it was to be used only by the patient.
>
> I was very young when the thing I am going to tell you about happened. I did not think anything about it at the time, as I was too young to know anything about such things. My brother was much

People from far and near asked Wolfkiller's grandfather to perform medicine ceremonies. This man appears to be determined although he lives under humble conditions.

older than I was. He was a medicine man. Our uncle, who knew all of the ceremonies, had taught him the chant that we use to dispel the evil spirits of war. He had his grandfather's medicine bag with all of the things in it that are to be used in this chant. Among the other things in the bag was a costume with a cap made of the skin of a coyote, with a snakeskin around it. There were bands made in the same way for the arms and legs and also a belt.

These things were to be used on a patient when he was ill from the effects of something he had seen in war, or if he had been bitten by a snake or had seen someone else bitten. There are many things the chant is used to cure the ill effects of, as you know.

As I said before, my brother had learned this chant, and when our uncle died, he got the medicine bag. He was called to perform ceremonies many times, and he did it well. Every time he performed a ceremony, the person he performed it for would forget his fears and would be well again. As you know, thinking too much about unpleasant things brings them on us.

My brother was always smiling, and he was happy and friendly toward everyone. All the people liked him.

When the first white soldiers we ever saw came to our hogan, my brother welcomed them and helped them as much as he could. They asked him to show them the things in his medicine bag. The man they had as an interpreter was a man my brother had seen before. My brother told us he was a good man, and my brother liked him.

When the chief of the soldiers saw the costume in the medicine bag, he asked my brother to put it on. My brother refused, and said he could not do it. He explained that it was only to be used in ceremonies, and then it was worn by the patient and not by the medicine man. The soldiers told him they understood how he felt about it, and they said no more about it that night. But the next day they again asked him to put it on and let them make a picture of him in it. He still refused. The soldiers camped near our hogans for several days, and every day they tried to persuade him to put the costume on. One day he finally consented. He put it on and let them make his picture.

After the soldiers left, my brother began to talk about what he had done. He said he knew he had done wrong and was worried about it. Soon he thought so much about it he could not sleep at

Hoops were placed in the ground in front of the hogan in preparation for the cleansing ceremony.

night. When he did sleep, he dreamed about the costume. Our people decided to have a chant for him to get his mind back in the path of peace.

After the ceremony was over, my brother felt better. He said he was going to bury the costume so no one else would ever have the trouble he had had because of it and so he could forget about it. He buried it under a rock on the mountain.

I had almost forgotten all about it, but since I saw my brother in the costume in my dreams last night, I must have a ceremony to dispel the evil thought from my mind. Your brother will go for a medicine man to perform the ceremony, and I want you to gather the plants.

Grandfather told me what plants were needed. I gathered them and had them all ready for the medicine man when he came four days later.

The next morning after he came, the ceremony began. It was to last four days.

The first day we were busy making hoops and arrows for the ceremony. We made four hoops, large enough for a person to crawl through—one of red willow, one of cedar, one of chokecherry, and one of wild rose. The medicine man lined these up on the east side of the hogan, just deep enough in the ground so they would stand. The red willow one was placed first, then the cedar, then the chokecherry, and then the one of wild rose almost at the door of the hogan. On the tops of the hoops he tied some eagle down.

By the time we had finished making the hoops and the medicine man had placed them in the ground, it was almost sunset. That is when the first day's ceremony must be performed. We went into the hogan.

The medicine man took a piece of white cloth and tied it on Grandfather with tufts of redtop grass. The first tie was at the forehead, the second at the breast, the third at the waist, and the fourth at the loins. The cloth covered him from head to foot all of the time this ceremony was being performed. During this part of the ceremony, the medicine man and the rest of the men in the hogan were chanting.

Then we went out of the hogan, still chanting. Grandfather knew what he was to do. He lay down on this stomach and crawled through the hoops. As he went through the first one, he broke the tie at his forehead to let the cloth slip off his head. Then he removed the eagle down from the hoop. As he went through the second one, he broke the tie at his breast and let the cloth slip from his shoulder, and removed the eagle down from that hoop. Then he went through the third one, and as he did, he broke the tie at his waist and removed the eagle down again. The white cloth slipped farther back, and by the time he was through the fourth hoop and the last tie was broken and the eagle down was taken from the last hoop, the cloth was left lying on the ground. The medicine man picked up the cloth and took it back into the hogan to be put in the medicine bag for use again the next day.

As soon as the ceremony was over, my mother and some of the other women brought our supper into the hogan. After we had eaten it, we sat around and talked for a while. Then the medicine man began to chant again, and the rest of the men joined in. The women sat around on the north side of the hogan until the chants were finished, which was a little after the middle of the night.

On the afternoon of the next day, the medicine man said some more prayers and chanted until almost sunset. Then he placed the hoops on the south side of the hogan, and the ceremony was again performed at sunset. On the third day, the hoops were placed on the west side of the hogan and the ceremony was performed again. On the fourth day, the hoops were placed on the north side of the hogan and the ceremony was performed for the final time.

Shortly after dark on the fourth day, two men were sent out to perform a ceremony with the arrows we had made. These arrows were made of yellow pine with the needles still on them. The arrows were painted black, and some eagle down was tied to the needles. The points were stone. One of the men went around the south side of the hogan to the west side. Then the man who stood at the door on the east side of the hogan threw his arrow over the hogan. The man on the west side then threw his arrow over the hogan. They then picked up the arrows, and the man on the east side passed to the south side. The man on the west side passed to the north side and threw his arrow over to the south. Then the other arrow was thrown to the north.

When this ceremony was finished, they met on the west side and combed the hogan with the arrows, all around to the door where they met again. Here they placed the arrows over the door to be left until the next morning.

The chanting went on all through the last night. At sunrise, the medicine man took the arrows from over the door. One of the arrow points was broken, but the other point was still whole. The points were taken out of the arrows, and the good one returned to the medicine bag. The broken point was taken with the arrows some distance to the east where they were placed under a small sage. They were sprinkled with pollen, and some prayers were said over them.

After the four-day ceremony was over and everyone had gone from our hogan, I asked Grandfather to tell me why he had crawled through the hoops, and what the white cloth was for.

"The white cloth is to represent the skin of a snake," he said, "and going through the hoops represents the snakes going into their holes. The cloth slipped from my body as the skins of the snake slips from his body. Every year he gets a new skin. The costume I told you about was used for this ceremony before it was buried. Now we use the white cloth in its stead."

I then asked him to tell me about the broken arrow point.

"When an arrow point is broken, it cannot be used again. It must be sprinkled with pollen, some prayers said, and the broken point left with the arrows when they are taken out to be put under the sage.

"If a mouse or any other animal were to run out of the dirt that covers the hogan while the men are combing it, they would spear it with the arrow point. Then there would be blood on the arrow. If this were to happen, the arrow would be taken to the north of the hogan where all evil goes, and it would be placed under the sage and sprinkled with pollen in the same way a broken arrow point would be taken to the east. The arrow point with the blood on it would be laid aside until the next night.

"At the same time of day that the arrow ceremony was performed the night before, the medicine man would paint the arrow point black as he painted me. The arrow point would be the same as a patient, and the prayers and chants sung over it. This ceremony would give the arrow point more power to find the evil spirit the next time it was used. The medicine man would put it in his medicine bag again after the ceremony was over."

The Long Trail

Three more years went by. Grandfather performed many ceremonies and taught me many things about them.

One morning he came to me. He looked happy and contented. We talked for a while about things around us. Then he said, "My grandson, I will not be with you much longer. I want you to remember what I have taught you and live your life. I am going on a long journey to the peaceful land at sunrise twenty days after this day."

I could not speak for a while after he said this. I was so sad to hear it. When I could speak again, I told him he must not talk like that. "You are still well and strong, my grandfather. Why do you want to leave us? We have tried to follow your teachings."

"My grandson," he said, "I am well pleased with you. You have not complained much about the few troubles you have had since the day when you were a little boy that I began to teach you about life. There are

Wolfkiller's grandfather faced his last days without fear. This deserted hogan provides a reminder of days past.

still many things for you to learn, but after I am gone, you can learn them by asking some of the older men and by your own observations. If you watch everything about you, you can understand many things. I want to tell you a little more about some of the plants and some of the ceremonies before I go. We will ride around and find the plants I want to tell you about. I want to see them again before I go."

"But what has put this thought into your mind?" I asked. "What have you seen or heard to cause you to say you are going away?"

"My brother came to me last night while I slept," he answered. "He told me he would come for me in twenty days. He said it would then be time for me to go, and he would be here at sunrise on that day. I am not sorry to go. I have had a full life and have been happy. I know the time will not seem too long before the ones I am leaving behind will go to me. I will miss all of you for a while, but I know the time is almost here for me to go, and I am glad I know just when it will be. I am not sad about it, my grandson, and I do not want you to grieve for me anymore than you can help. Just think how much better it is for me to go now while I am still strong than it would be if it was my lot to stay here until I was so old that I would be helpless."

When we reached the hogan that evening, my mother was very sad, and I knew that Grandfather had told her the things he had told me. She did not say anything about it, though. She tried to be cheerful, and when Grandfather came in, she talked to him as if nothing had happened.

For several days, as we rode around together, I could hardly see my way because my eyes were full of tears. I felt so helpless when I looked at Grandfather, but I tried to do what he wanted me to do. We rode together to the different places where the plants grew and to the other places he said he wanted to see before he went.

I said I wished I could go with him.

"My grandson, you must never say or think anything like that. It will make you too weak to live your life, and the best years are ahead of you. You are not the one to say when you should take the long trail. We must not talk about this thing anymore. I am ready to go, but you have many things to do before you go."

The last few days, we stayed around the hogan and Grandfather talked to the family. After the children put the sheep in the corral at night, he told them the stories he had told me when I was a little boy. He said that I must remember the stories so I could pass them on to the children when he was gone.

"My grandson, you may sometimes come to places in your life when you will be tempted to leave the path of light. We all come to places of that kind in the course of our lives. I want you to promise me that you will always follow the path you know you should follow. The path of life is like the trails we ride. Sometimes we come to places where the trail forks. One trail leads over the smooth rock where you can barely see it. In such places, there are only a few white marks and the rock is worn a little to let you know that other people have been over it. If you take that fork, it will lead you out into the open flat and to the place you are trying to get to. The other trail looks much smoother and is very plain, but it leads you into many places where the canyons are deep and dark and the trails are more rough and rocky than the trail you should have taken."

On the morning of the day before my grandfather was to go, he got up before dawn. I went out of the hogan with him. We stood watching the dawn. The first streak came white and clear. We stood there watching it as it grew whiter and whiter. I looked at him when the first red streaks of the sun began to come. He stood watching, but said nothing until the sun came bright and clear through the curtains and the mountains began to turn blue. "I wanted to see it again before I go," he said. "I am glad it is to be a beautiful day."

We went back into the hogan as soon as the sun was above the mountains. Mother had our breakfast ready for us, but I was so sad that I could not eat. Grandfather was cheerful, and he ate and talked as if nothing was to happen. He spoke about the people and things around the country until after the middle of the day. No one said anything about what was to happen the next day.

As the sun was dipping toward the west, Grandfather said, "My grandson, I want you and your father and your sister's husband to put this borrowed body in the lap of our Mother Earth when the spirit is gone from it. I will tell you now about the burial ceremony. You have seen some of it, but I have not told you why we do the things we do. The first day and night after one dies, the spirit goes around the body with the wind. The second day and night it goes around with the spirit of the dark. On the third day and night it goes around with the spirit of the dawn. On the fourth and last day it goes around on the wings of the sun or the moon. An owl, a whippoorwill, the spirit of the dawn, or the spirit of the night will come to take the spirit of the person to the peaceful land. When the four circles are complete, the one who comes for the spirit will either take it on the wings of the sun or the moon. It depends on what time of day or night the spirit is ready to go. If it is while the sun is in the sky, it will go on the wings of the sun, but if the moon is in the sky, it goes on the wings of the moon. If you have not lived this life right and a coyote or a mouse comes for the spirit, it is bad. As when we go in bad company to the other land, we will not be received very well

"The reason the people who perform the burial ceremony jump over a cactus, a yucca plant, and an anthill the fourth day after the spirit is ready to go is so the spirit will not follow them back. That is why we all carry the little bag of pebbles from an anthill. You know that we throw them at any noise that startles us when we are compelled to camp at a place after dark. We may be camped where someone had just died, and we would not want their spirit to come near us."

We sat out in front of the hogan and Grandfather talked to the family until the middle of the night. Then he said he wanted to sleep where he could see the stars and the moon this last night. As soon he lay down, he went to sleep, but I did not sleep. I lay by his side and watched him until the dawn came. Then he sat up and watched the dawn with me. Just before the sun came, he lay down again.

Just as the sun came over the mountains, he said, "Goodbye, my children. I must be going now."

We all began to grieve for him when he stopped breathing.

All of the family left that place and carried with them all of their clothes and the other things into the hogan. They went a short distance from the hogan and sat down with their blankets over their heads to wait for the three of us who were to bury the body to come back from the grave.

We bathed the body and dressed it in the best clothes and put the moccasins on the wrong feet. It must be done that way so it will not make the same kind of tracks as one of us who are left behind would make. We took off all of our clothes except our loincloths and let our hair fall around us. With the ashes and soot from some plants we had burned, we painted our bodies. The plants were some that we used in the ceremonies. Then we got his horse, saddled and bridled it, and put his body across the saddle. Two of us walked on the sides of the horse to hold the body while the other one led the horse.

We took the body to the north of the hogan, where we built a small hogan of poles under the rocks. Into this, we put the body. We broke the beads and other things he had on and tore holes in his clothes. Then we broke the saddle, cut the bridle, and mashed the bit with stones so the spirit of the thought that had been put in the making of those things would go with him to the other land. We put the saddle, bridle, and ropes into the grave with the body. After we closed the grave, we killed the horse with stones.

When this was done, we went back to the hogan, walking single file. Mother had put a jug of water near the hogan. When we reached it, we bathed our bodies and washed our hair with yucca. We kept very close together, as nothing must pass between us for four days and nights. After we bathed, the people could eat. It was getting toward the middle of the day before we had our breakfast.

The family could not be with the three of us until after the four days passed. We had our own campfires near the hogan. The rest of the family was a short distance from us where they, too, must stay for four days. We guarded the trail we had made when we took the body to bury it. Nothing must cross the trail until after sunset for the four days and nights. Two of us could sleep at a time, but one of us must be on guard.

We did not talk much. I thought a great deal about my grandfather and the things he had taught me. "It will be hard for me to go on without him," I thought, but I knew what I must do. I still had my mother and father—they would help me.

When the fourth day had passed, the three of us went back to the grave to say the final prayer. My father knew what we were to say. When we reached the grave, he told us to repeat after him the things he said:

Now you go on your way alone;
What you now are, we know not;
To what clan you now belong we know not;
From now on, you are not of this earth.

When this was finished, we went back to the hogan, jumping over anthills, yucca plants, and cactus as we went. When we reached the hogan, we took some poles out of its north side so other people who might pass that way would know that no one was to enter it or camp

Wolfkiller grieved over the loss of his grandfather but found strength in the enduring landscape.

near it. By the hole in it, they would know the spirit of death had been there. If someone had died inside of a hogan, the body would have been taken out through the hole. It would have been made when the body was ready for burial. Because Grandfather had died outside, we did not make the hole until the four days were up.

As soon as we finished with this part of the ceremony, we took a sweat bath. Then we bathed our bodies in cold water and washed our hair. When this was done, we joined the rest of the family. We could now mingle with the other people.

That day we moved from that place, and our lives went on as before.

PLANTS	USES	CHANTS INDIAN	CHANTS ENGLISH
No. 1 I-ní ilchkoch Lightning emotic Pentstemoneatoni	Used in case one is struck or stunned by lightning, also used for stomach trouble and backache.	Nat-o-i Bi-kank zilchkidji At-sos Yo-I Klezhi	Male wound Mountain Feather or veir Bead Night
No. 2 Na-o-kos be-ilchkoch Great dipper emetic or Spirit of the north	This is used in case one is troubled by evil spirits. or for general disorders of the body.	Zilchkidii yo-i Klezhi	Mountain Bead Night
No. 8 Na-shoi di-chizhi il-chi Like a horned toad Aquilegia caerulea	Used to stop hemmorrnages.	Ma-i	Coyote
No. 10 Ma-i kle-zhin nat-o Black fox tobacco Artemisiatridentata	To cure the bite of the Water snake.	Itsa-ji To-i	Eagle Water
No. 11 Ta-ilch-ka di-jadi bi-nat-o Tobacco of the water spider. Penothera muitijuga	Used in case of one having bad dreams of water, being hurt, or dreaming of being hurt by hail stones.	Nelódi To-i	Hail Water
No. 14 Tipetan Sheep food	To cure headache, toothache or sore throat.	Át-sos	Feather or Vein
No, 15 Na-shoi bi-nat-O Rattle snake tobacco Oenotheuasp	Used to sprinkle on medicine things and sand painting also in chants.	Di-ná bi-nálchiji Nat-o-i Ba-ád Nat-o-i Bi-kank	Navajo wind Female wound male wound
No. 16 Pí il-de Deer horns	Used by the Navajos when they go on a hunt.	Át-sos	Feather or Vein
No. 19 Bi tan ziz-kai White edged leaves— King Fisher Medicine	Used to cure gun shot wounds, also to keep down fever.	Zilchkidji	Mountain

Page 1

Wolfkiller showed Louisa Wetherill the native plants that were significant to the Navajos and explained how they were used for food and medicine. This is an index page from Louisa Wetherill's ethnobotanical specimen chest. An analysis of her material was published in *The Ethnobotany of the Kayenta Navajo*, by Leland C. Wyman and Stuart K. Harris, after her death.

EPILOGUE

By Louisa Wade Wetherill

As the years went by, Wolfkiller visited us often, and we spent many evenings in conversation. During the summers, he would not talk of much except plants. "That is when the lightning and snakes are awake," he explained. During the winters, he would tell me about all subjects of interest to me, including history, ceremonies, and the lessons of life.

When he went out to gather plants, Wolfkiller often took me along. He showed me how they should be gathered if they were to be used in a ceremony and taught me how herbs were used for healing. This knowledge, he explained, was not really a secret one, but was a science that required many years of study. Based on this information, I gathered, pressed, and cataloged over three hundred specimens of herbs used by the medicine men.

During the winter of 1920–21, Wolfkiller and Hosteen Luka accompanied my husband and me on a trip to southern Arizona. We ventured down into Mexico in search of evidence that some of the Navajo clans might have lived there in the early days. Back in Arizona, we found a ranch just north of the border where we could start a winter operation. After four years of preparation, we opened Hacienda de la Osa for guests in 1924. Wolfkiller again came south with us to serve as our wrangler and handyman.

For the twenty years I knew Wolfkiller, I never saw him angry or disturbed by anything that might cause someone else to show emotion, nor did I ever know him to tell a lie. He lived his religion and kept on working right up to the end. One day he brought the sheep back to the corral in the late afternoon. An hour later, he was gone. He died as he had lived—quietly and in peace with the world.

Riding in the Tucson parade. (Front to back) Louisa Wetherill, John Yazzie, Wolfkiller, Mrs. Joe, and John Wetherill. Wolfkiller also went by the name "George" during this period.

DIAMONDS
GREENWALD
& ADAMS

Preparing for the trip from La Osa to Kayenta, ca 1925. (Left to right) Wolfkiller, Mrs. Joe, John Yazzie (climbing into car), Betty and Fanny Wetherill (foster daughters), John Wetherill, Ben Wetherill, and Georgia Wetherill Kilcrease (in background).